COMPETITIVE GOVERNMENT

COMPETITIVE GOVERNMENT

Delivering Excellence

CHRIS PRIOR

First published 2014
Copyright © 2016 by Chris Prior

All rights reserved

www.competitivegovernment.com

Cover image: ©Ace_Create–iStockphoto.com
©Milagli–shutterstock.com

No part of this book may be used or reproduced in any manner whatsoever without written permission of the author except in the case of brief quotations embedded in critical articles or reviews.

Third edition

10 9 8 7 6 5 4 3 2

For Lily and Cosmo

CONTENTS

PROLOGUE 9

WHY GOVERNMENT MATTERS 13

GOVERNMENT AND COMPETITION 19

THE NATURE OF COMPETITION 31

DELIVERING WINNING GOVERNMENT 43

Winning public support 45

Enterprising government 52

Excellent people 63

WINNING POLICIES 71

Budgets and taxes 72

Education 80

Health care 87

Welfare 96

Pensions 103

Defense 105

Law enforcement 111

Civil society 119

Infrastructure 125

Commerce and agriculture 130

EPILOGUE 135

PROLOGUE

Competitive Government is a small book about a big idea.

Few would associate the words competitive and government, yet most want their government to be excellent. The question is how to achieve it? The premise behind this book is that governments fail because they lack a mechanism to ensure they succeed. This is competitive government; it is the new philosophy of government.

Over the centuries, much has been written about the nature of government, who should run it, and to whom it should be accountable. Very little thought has been given to ensuring that it operates as efficiently and effectively as possible. Government has inexorably expanded, acquiring new responsibilities and commitments, without any idea how to guarantee its policies and programs give the best value for money on a continuing basis.

The result is that government is underperforming. The vigor and dynamism of previous decades has been replaced by torpor and paralysis. Instead of advancing, in many countries it is festering, and starting to decay. Challenges remain and evolve, but too frequently government is seen as part of the problem, not part of the solution. Successes and progress are achieved in spite of, rather than because of, government involvement. Improving the performance of government is the "elephant in the room" when it comes to addressing issues of national decline, and seeking ways to generate new prosperity and economic growth.

Government is too important to be allowed to fail. Every citizen and corporation needs government to perform at its best, the task is to ensure that it does. Habitually, when uncompetitive government gets into difficulty, the standard response of politicians is to try to reduce expenditure, to curtail services, to talk about tightening belts and austerity, while looking for ways to borrow more money and to disguise tax increases. The results of this piecemeal approach are seldom satisfactory. What is new and innovative tends to be cut, what is old and inefficient tends to remain. Halfhearted and superficial attempts are made at reform, but rarely is any significant improvement actually achieved. Extra burdens are imposed; government becomes worse not better. Instead what is required are not knee jerk responses or a plethora of short term initiatives, but a new paradigm that addresses the issue of maximizing government performance once and for all – competitive government.

Competitive government is a modus operandi that applies to everything that government does or seeks to achieve. It is not some narrow contracting out or outsourcing exercise, but about injecting competition into the very heart of government. In essence, it concerns how to make a country as prosperous, and as attractive place to live as possible. It embraces not just the efficiency of government administration, but more importantly, how good its policies and programs are in adding and leveraging the most value to its society.

Competitive government applies to government at all levels, not just national but supra national, regional and local. The principles of competitive government will be eventually adopted by all at some point. Few citizens want an underperforming government. Countries sink slowly at first, failing governments may limp on for years, but ultimately, they condemn themselves. Governments either choose or will be forced to become more competitive. How it happens and when, is crucial. It is something that you can influence and shape. It is in your interests that it occurs as rapidly and painlessly as possible. It almost goes without saying, but the benefits that come from having a winning government, far exceed those offered by a losing government. For corporations, improving government is a key contributor to increasing profitability and investor returns.

Winning governments demonstrate very high levels of citizen

satisfaction. They deliver first class public services, supported by tax regimes that foster prosperity, with regulations that enhance national performance. Success requires fundamental changes in the way government operates, what it seeks to do and how it delivers. As part of the process it becomes agile, enterprising and dynamic; it adopts best practices, facilitates choices, takes risks and innovates in its policies and programs. Winning governments ensure that they are at the center of a virtuous cycle of improvement, that is not only self-sustaining, but mutually reinforcing.

Inherent in competition is liberty. Competitive government cannot be sustained without a society and a political system that supports choice. The success of government rooted in democracy, with a liberal philosophy of individual freedom, equal rights for men and women, a broadly capitalist economy with a preference for free trade, is widely recognized. Those who deny, or seek to limit options, who repress information, that reject transparency, who stifle innovation cannot produce truly competitive governments. Indispensable are competing views; the freedom to debate different ideas or ways of doing things, and to make good or bad choices.

The presumption that government should be of the people, by the people, and for the people is inseparable from competitive government. Totalitarian, authoritarian and repressive regimes may in the short term match or exceed the performance of democratic countries in some areas; but by denying the freedoms essential to competition, they cannot achieve lasting success and become victims of their internal contradictions. Countries that are so blighted need to find a way to throw off the yoke before they can even consider becoming competitive. Competitive government, however, holds out the torch of hope for those who yearn for change; the better competitive governments do, the more exposed and isolated bad governments become. This book is not about "rotten" or fragmenting governments other than to observe that nature abhors a vacuum and that such regimes are very dangerous not only for their own citizens, but for the international community as a whole, and demand collective action to address and resolve.

Democracy on its own does not secure competitive government. Positive outcomes matter, just voting is not enough. If governments do not have the power, resources or competence to deliver what the people want, are promised or expect, then confidence in the process is severely eroded. The razzmatazz of political campaigns is no substitute for effectiveness, a cycle of elections no guarantee of performance when in office.

The focus of this book is inevitably on "developed" governments but it is also highly relevant to "developing" nations. A country with a relatively poor government infrastructure and limited resources, can make rapid progress by learning from the mistakes of the more "mature" countries; potentially leapfrogging them in the delivery of competitive government. I am painfully conscious that I have not got all the answers. I am drawn to the notion that a book is more like an app that gets updated and improved over time. To help achieve this I am very grateful for contributions and observations that strengthen its argument and content. I have standardized on American spellings and referred to money in dollars.

I have not aimed to write an academic textbook or a political diatribe. I have deliberately produced a short book that is easy to read and accessible, without numerous footnotes and references. This is not a negation of scholarship, but a reflection of the view that weighty tomes, especially on government tend to put off readers, and their content becomes dated and increasingly irrelevant. Inevitably the text is conditioned by the year in which it was written, but it is my belief that the ideas behind competitive government will stand the test of time.

Chris Prior
Oxford 2016

WHY GOVERNMENT MATTERS

Government matters because depending on where you live, it spends at least 30% and in many cases considerably more of what you earn. Invariably, as it finds it hard to raise all the money it consumes, it also borrows enormous sums on your behalf. The quality of the services it provides effect every aspect of your life. How well your government performs is of vital importance to your happiness and wellbeing.

Given its vast reach, imagine the benefits you would gain if your government gave greater value. You could be thousands of dollars better off, corporations would be more successful, and your country more prosperous. Even the most hardened defender of the status quo would find it hard to argue that no scope existed for improvement. The question is not whether, but how much? Understanding the potential for this, and providing a mechanism for it to be realized, is what competitive government is all about.

Of course, it is easy to be critical. Most of what gets written about government is hostile; it is far harder to be supportive and creative. This book is unashamedly pro-government. The arguments about the need for government have been had and won. Without it, in some form, the life of man would indeed be in Thomas Hobbes's phrase, "solitary, poor, nasty, brutish, and short." With it, the task is to ensure that it actively makes people happier, richer, safer and healthier. Defining and delivering government's mission is central to competitive government. Indeed, forgetting the fundamentals of what government is there to achieve, lies at the heart of its problems, and presents one of the major challenges that must be addressed for it to improve.

So why bother and why now? It is true that for many, government is seen as benign, flawed and wasteful perhaps, but nothing to get too worried about. That is until something starts to go seriously wrong. In several countries, that point has already been reached, and unless action is taken, things will only get worse.

Paradoxically, if growth is any measure, then government has been spectacularly successful in the twentieth century. Yet it is precisely this triumph that has sown the seeds of its vulnerability. Indeed, modern government might be seen as a victim of its own success, and the expectations placed upon it. Government expenditure started to increase in the late nineteenth century with the introduction of limited welfare measures. It took off after World War I on a trend that meant that by the start of World War II, it had more than doubled, with it doubling again by 1980. On average, public sector employment has gone up six times, employing approximately a fifth of the working population. In some countries government is larger, in some smaller, but the pattern is familiar in every developed country. There are a number of reasons for this expansion. This book is not the place to document the past in detail. What is fair to say is that it happened without any map, model or destination in mind. No one set out with a master plan, a view of what was the ideal size and scope of government and how to get there. Growth was reactive and consequential, more haphazard than deliberate.

Government was held in high regard. Popular faith in the power of it to do good was strong. If there was a problem, an inequality, an abuse, then all that was necessary was for government to expand to address the issue and all would be fine.

For a time this worked, and worked well. Starting from a green field site, it was relatively easy to make an impact and claim success. As the decades have passed, however, it has proved increasingly hard to maintain performance. Public sector productivity has lagged and spiraled downward. It is as if government is like a person, it has become aged and obese, lacking the energy and the spark to act, its libido gone, arteries clogged and vital organs diseased.

The results are evident, ask yourself a few questions. Are the services you receive worth what they cost, or put another way, could your money be better spent? How good is government's customer service, and how does it compare with other organizations? When you consider what you buy with what you have left after taxes, (food, clothes, housing, energy, insurance, vacations, transportation; all purchased at prices inflated by sales taxes, government policies, regulations and duties), and in some cases having to make private provision to compensate for the failings of public services, questioning the value you get from government becomes ever more pressing.

Even this challenge is a little academic, as very few people (including those in government) know what its services and regulations actually cost, or indeed, how much tax (when every tax is taken into account) citizens are really paying. Add to this public borrowing, together with a sea of unfunded promises and obligations, and assessing the value added of government becomes virtually impossible. Increasingly, people do not want to pay more, but they do not want to get even less. The old solution of raising taxes to do new things is no longer acceptable, likewise it is very difficult to shut down existing programs to release resources for new requirements. Instead, uncompetitive governments resort to massive borrowing to keep reality at bay. Amassing ever larger burdens of debt, without any idea how such debts will be repaid, postpones, rather than addresses the denouement that at some point has to be faced.

Government has entered a phase in its evolution where it appears unable to change and be dynamic. This situation affects all, conservatives are unable to significantly contract its role, and liberals are unable to get it to modernize to take on new functions. The sense of drift is palpable. The position is unsustainable and very wasteful of the power and potential of government. Sooner or later, something has to give. Numerous attempts have been made to reverse government's decline, unfortunately all have sunk without trace. Countless politicians have tried to deliver major reform, all have failed. The challenge is not only to initiate change, but also to make it endure beyond the political life of the instigator. Those elected with high ideals are thwarted by the nature of the government machine. Instead of sitting in the driving seat, they are gradually taken hostage by the system, becoming little more than pawns for a bureaucracy that they theoretically control. Conditioned to what is possible, rather than reforming government, it reforms them. Slowly resignation sets in, their efforts relegated to the margins of public policy, a tweak here and there, but not much else. Frustrated by what they see; the good, the able, the talented do not become politicians or enter public service. The very checks and balances that hundreds of years ago seemed so sensible to avoid the abuse of power and corruption, lead to a different form of evil, that of sloth and waste. Often government fails at the simplest of tasks. Things are not improved because it is all too difficult to change. Anything that does happen happens incredibly slowly, at great expense, with little appreciable impact or benefit. This inertia has many causes, the cumulative effect however, is growing public disillusionment and dissatisfaction with both the democratic and governmental process.

Democratic countries pride themselves on universal suffrage. Regular elections are held, and in theory, people are free to elect anyone who they want to rule them. Yet this is only one side of democracy. Democracy, rule of the people, is far more than just voting, it is about the actual delivery of promises made during the elections. Without this substance, the democratic process is mere theatre. The challenge is having the competence to do this thereby addressing the sense of popular powerlessness that results from the failure of government to deliver. Uncompetitive government is too "big" to deal with small scale issues where it can make a real difference such as dealing with social nuisance, litter and the provision of restrooms which citizens find it very hard to address individually but too "small" to deliver on the promises made during campaigns. Democracy requires agility and results, it demands action as well as words. To make it real, it needs the ability to harness the resources of government to deliver the outcomes people have voted for. The absence of this is not only dangerous, the fatalism that it engenders condones government's continued poor performance.

Typically losing government provides defense that fails to defend against real threats, law enforcement that fails to deal with crime, education that fails to be outstanding, health services that fail to promote health, social security that fails to provide decent pensions, and welfare that fails to facilitate improved welfare; all largely financed through taxation systems that are horrendously complex, and do little to encourage the creation of wealth and prosperity. The ultimate spiral of decline is fueled by government developing new policies and programs to tackle failures in existing ones which are allowed to remain in force. Evidence based policy making is ignored, resources are not prioritized, hard decisions are not made and good opportunities are lost. Poor policies like poor products, designed badly and administered inefficiently make you worse off. Countries with uncompetitive governments fail to attract investment and spur companies to move elsewhere, so fostering still further deterioration.

Government is far too important to be written off. The resources it consumes, the responsibilities it shoulders, and the impact it can have, mean that it cannot be neglected or sidelined. The need for government has not gone away, the potential benefits of what good government can achieve are massive, and the opportunities are there to be realized if only the nature of government can change to grasp them. The tragedy for many countries is that there is much that their governments can do to make them better and more prosperous, if only the will was present, the direction clear and the mechanism existed to deliver. Just because government is as it is, it does not mean it is as it should be. For those who really care about public service action is imperative, for every day of delay is another day of tolerating waste and decay. To address the challenge is not easy but nothing worthwhile is ever straight forward. What is required is a new approach, one that provides a framework for enduring improvement. Competitive government is all embracing, it is based on a hardnosed reality that cannot be ignored, and will ultimately succeed, where other initiatives or models have failed or been shown wanting.

GOVERNMENT AND COMPETITION

For some the idea of competitive government is an oxymoron, a contradiction in terms. Government, it is argued is sovereign, it is by definition a monopoly, without competitors or rivals. This view is fundamentally flawed but is at the root of government's underperformance.

What is true about government and competition is that until very recently, governments have been able to shelter the evaluation of their domestic performance behind their perceived monopoly status. As a result, they have had little incentive to worry about the value of the services they offer and citizen satisfaction. It is ironic that some governments vigorously pursue antitrust actions against alleged commercial monopolies and monopolistic practises, yet palpably ignore the impact of monopoly on their own performance and value for money.

Even if private monopolies are not broken up, over time they become victims of their own complacency, and failing to respond to change, they wither and die. Government it is held is different, so it just carries on; rolling over and adding to its inadequacies from one decade to the next. Its citizens little more than virtual prisoners of its underperforming policies and programs, resigned to muddling through the best they can.

In truth government has always been subject to competition, but the nature of this competition is changing dramatically. The old competitive forces of military rivalry and ideological certainty are in steady decline. The new competition is not a series of events such as battles, revolutions and elections, it is ongoing and much more deep-seated. It concerns how to best deliver and maintain efficient and effective government that adds and leverages the most value for citizens and corporations.

Armed conflicts have not been eliminated, but for most countries, the specter of military competition resulting in a general military conflagration is increasingly remote. While the need for vigilance remains, the nature of the threat, and the challenge presented, is less obvious than at any time in modern history. It is not so much because mankind has changed, but that technology has altered the calculus; any national aggressor would stand to lose far more than they could expect to gain. Countries simply cannot afford war, the dreadful horror of its human toll is no longer acceptable or tolerable. Governments must not ignore new dangers ranging from violence from terrorists, state sponsored separatists and proxies, criminals, religious fanatics and failing states, to governments and non-governmental groups using nonphysical aggression to secure objectives. While these challenges require highly competitive and agile responses, they are in a totally different league from the conflicts or potential conflicts that dominated the twentieth century.

In democracies, the political battle over ideas has also significantly changed. Gone are the days when countries faced radical choices between socialism, communism and capitalism. Indeed, the blurring of agendas between political parties means that it is quite possible to have a "socialist" or "liberal" espousing what might be seen as "conservative" policies and vice versa.

In most developed countries, the actual difference in policy terms between the main parties is minuscule. Consensus reigns, there is broad agreement about most policies, and sheer practicality gets in the way of chopping and changing programs. Elections are about tweaking at the margins, the focus is on an initiative here, or there, rather than wholesale change.

The old competitive forces often reduced the pressure for scrutiny of the effectiveness of national governments. If you are worried about apocalyptic conflict, or believe that the problems of government are going to be addressed once you get rid of the evil socialists or capitalists in power, and undertake a wholesale replacement of their political ideology, then the intricate analysis of how effectively government actually operates and the value for money that it delivers, seems of secondary importance. Once nightmares of Armageddon or visions of Utopia have been removed, it is only a matter of time before popular gaze starts to focus on the relative performance of government; how well it meets the expectations of taxpayers, and how its services compare with those elsewhere? Inexorably, these challenges will prove far more enduring agents for change than aggression or ideology.

Competitive government encompasses a new type of competition, one that is still in its formative stages. It centers not so much on the achieving of power but the "boring reality" of how to exercise it in the most effective way. The transition is away from direct physical competition to a more comprehensive and fundamental challenge of governmental competence, with at its heart, the delivery of policies and programs that add maximum value. The issue has moved on from debating the ownership of the ship of state, to the nature of the vessel itself, its direction, how it is managed and run. It is about its performance in comparison to others, and whether it could operate any better?

The crux of the argument is that governments face emerging competitive forces that can only be confronted successfully by becoming more competitive themselves. To respond effectively, to offer the best services to their citizens, governments have to embrace competition, harness choice and focus on the maximization of citizen satisfaction. They must want to win, to beat their competitors both within and outside their countries to deliver what their people value most.

Vital is the recognition that unresponsive governments have no special or protected status, they can and will fail. Bad government does not have to prevail. Bankruptcy, collapse and default are extremely painful, but ultimately an essential, cathartic process from which a winning government, phoenix like, can emerge. As it is with nature, so it is with government. The idea that somehow governments are immune from the consequences of failure, that public debt is a rock solid investment and that future promises of entitlements are inviolable, is erroneous and unsustainable. Smaller states can be bailed out for a while, but can easily become an unsupportable burden, hastening the demise of bigger failing governments, and eroding the competitiveness of others.

Implicit in this text is a belief that competition is a good thing and that being competitive, and wanting to succeed is a worthy objective. Some will completely disavow this view, this book is not for them. There are many more who are suspicious of competition, and think there must be a better path. They should read on, for the argument propounded is that although it can be argued that competition is inherently wasteful, in the absence of certainty over the right way of doing things, competition offers the best chance of delivering the highest value from government. It is a dynamic force that benefits everyone: citizens, businesses, government employees and the economy as a whole. It improves services, it keeps costs and taxes down, and it fosters innovation and productivity, while reinforcing accountability.

Competitive government can be seen as both a threat and an opportunity. It is a threat because it requires and anticipates change and cannot be ignored. It is an opportunity, because it provides a philosophy to help all those who are serious about making government better. It encapsulates what is needed for progress, supplying the missing keystone essential for the successful reform and ongoing reinvigoration of government. Failing governments ultimately have to respond to its message whether they like it or not. Governments that seek to disregard the challenge condemn their citizens to relatively lower standards of provision, and a poorer quality of life. Attempting to resist it will ends in failure.

Sovereignty has been seen as a bulwark against competition. If countries could live in splendid isolation, if they could hide behind impenetrable borders and erect physical barriers, then they could make laws and administer themselves as the rulers saw fit, without regard to other nations. Some have tried to exercise this concept, even to the extent of autarky. All have found that it impoverishes their people and weakens the State. Indeed, experience has shown that the wealthiest are those that are most open to others; that embrace new ideas, people, products and services, and the advantages of free trade.

In reality the notion of complete sovereignty is an illusion. Countries have always dealt with each other and been influenced by the actions of others but until recently, governments were able to keep such interference at arm's length. In the latter half of the twentieth century, however, sovereignty has been eroded intentionally and unintentionally as never before. For defense, economic and political reasons, nations have formed deep alliances and unions that have effectively undermined their independence. The growth of multinational businesses, trade, technology, foreign investment and migration has further underlined the mutual dependence of states. National languages are waning, cultures are merging and tastes converging. All nations are faced with global problems ranging from environmental challenges, to the spread of disease. The decline of sovereignty has lowered, and in many cases removed, the barriers to competition. Arguably, the fifteenth century creation of the nation state met its nemesis at the beginning of the twenty first century.

Governments are extremely complex but that does not mean that they should be oblivious to performance, immune from innovation and progress. In commerce such stimulus comes from the desire to make money, the threat of new entrants, and the imperative not to go out of business. The pursuit of customer satisfaction spurs improvement, better products and the delivery of greater value. So it should be with government.

Governments and countries differ widely but they have similar objectives. It is a premise of this book that every government has the scope to become more competitive. Just as it is very unlikely that one government has all the answers, so another will not have all the problems. There is much to observe and analyze, some governments are worse at some things, others are better. It is vital that this examination is performed, and countries learn lessons and seek to apply best practice. Overall, if your government is less competitive, takes more and delivers less, then you are more likely to be impoverished compared with someone whose government is more competitive, takes relatively less but delivers proportionately more. Your government is failing you in its primary duty of fostering and developing prosperity for the future.

The argument is not about big versus small government; it is about determining what works and what does not. It is in the nature of competition that there are different sizes of government; the crucial factor is which is the most competitive and effective way government can leverage the greatest value to society. The principle of leverage, that of multiplying the impact of each tax dollar spent must be at the heart of decision taking and the evaluation of activities. Using outlays to seed desired outcomes through creating incentives, providing a mixture of carrots and sticks, can not only be cheaper and more effective than direct provision, it can help sculpt the shape of government itself. Smaller governments facilitate services; bigger governments actually provide them. If a government cannot deliver a service that is better than others, then it should withdraw, letting its competitors take over, or it should radically redesign its offering to make it competitive.

The debate focuses on competence, how to secure the best outcomes and highest satisfaction, not who manages the inputs or the physical delivery of the service. There are varying interpretations of the role of government and its ultimate responsibilities. Within this, however, it is vital not to get too hung up on established views of what is, and what is not "right" for government to do. There is a sliding scale between public and private provision varying from jurisdiction to jurisdiction. The question is not whether the cat is black or white, it is whether it catches mice?

Some governments, for instance, choose to provide health care, some do not. The key challenge is what option secures the most competitive outcome for its people? If it does provide healthcare, it is vital that government delivers best value, and that its citizens do not suffer from substandard treatment, or even have to pay again for the private sector to supply what the State promised to deliver. Likewise, as government has the ultimate responsibility for law enforcement, it should be effective at stopping crime. This requires thinking outside the traditional law enforcement box, but it means that individuals not having to endure the triple whammy of taxes, higher insurance premiums, and actual loss or personal trauma.

If the philosophy of competitive government is to be government's savior, its midwife is undoubtedly technology both as a messenger of relative performance and an enabler of change. First, information, ideas and commerce have become global breaking down barriers and creating opportunities. Second, information technology has revolutionized the environment in which government operates. Third, advances in medical, scientific and manufacturing processes has, and will have, a dramatic impact on government programs. Indeed, these technologies are just the start, human inventiveness and innovation is being unleashed at a phenomenal and unprecedented rate.

With the broader implications of globalization, technology is a vital element in helping to assess and judge the relative performance of national governments; enabling and empowering corporations, and increasingly individuals to make more informed choices and demand better. For most of what government does, it is impossible to hide behind what remains of sovereignty. Of course, cultural differences endure, but the notion that somehow a people are different, and do not need to have a competitive government because inefficiency and poor public services are an endearing national characteristic, is fanciful in the extreme. If uncompetitive governments fail to improve then they fall behind other governments that are more alert to the challenges and opportunities competition brings.

Technology has a profound bearing on how the private sector does business, the same ought to apply to government. Traditionally government has seen technology just as an adjunct to the way it operates, however, in the future it will dramatically change the whole nature of government itself. Most governments are only at the end of what might be termed the first stage in their use of technology. When IT was initially introduced, government and business did so at approximately the same time. Both required similar technology to automate clerical processes. Whereas for corporations, under competitive pressure, it was used to give a better service, to speed up product lifecycles, to boost productivity, to cut costs and become more efficient; for government, perceiving no such competitive imperative, it was seen as a device to sustain bureaucratic policies and procedures that had already become onerous, and even to make policies more complex and involved. Typically, the introduction of technology in the public sector has not been associated with any significant rationalization in the total number of staff employed or in the operation of government programs. Such outcomes have been explained away by reassuring statements that technology has kept staffing levels from actually rising, and that any extra resource released has been redeployed and channeled into other areas.

Used well, technology drives simplification. As businesses have streamlined, their requirements have changed, and technology has evolved accordingly. Corporations have moved away from large scale clerical operations, developing responsive business models that are more focused on dealing with the individual needs of customers. Government has actually changed very little. Hence when it comes to replacing technology, losing government is wedded to the past with outdated requirements, whereas businesses are looking to the future. Government can still be provided with its technology at a price, but it is significantly different from what efficient corporations are using and paying.

What most governments fail to appreciate is the extent to which developments in technology exposes their operations and policies to new forms of competition. They are as revolutionary to government practice as the printing press was to religious control in the Middle Ages. Not only does equipment and processes become obsolete, the "middle man" type functions that comprise much of the nature of government bureaucracy just do not need to exist. To be competitive, government needs not only to catch up, but to think ahead. It is simply unsustainable to retain the old-fashioned ways of working with new technology. New policy options open up that allow and require government to treat citizens as individuals rather than vast amorphous clusters to be administered centrally. Winning governments mine their data to make smarter decisions and achieve better outcomes from their programs.

The nature of the technology is such that it, and the skills to run it, are normally far more effectively and economically purchased from outside governments, than provided from within it. Best practice becomes global, rather than reinventing the wheel, competitive governments seek to harness existing solutions that are proven to deliver. Comparisons are assisted by outsourcing, with national governments engaging the same corporations, using the same technologies, doing fundamentally the same things, but with potentially significantly different overall costs and results.

The convergence between public and private technology gives the opportunity to compare and contrast actual performance in ways previously considered impossible. The relative cost of the failure of a government to adapt, and successfully compete, becomes more and more visible. This might have mattered little in the old world where governments did not see themselves in competition, but in the new, it is increasingly important to national prosperity.

Technology, is a double edged sword, the presumption is that government chooses to use it for good rather than ill. For instance, the capacity to identify and deal with threats before they are dangerous is a vital intelligence tool that should be used to spur much greater efficiency in the traditional apparatus of national security and law enforcement. Against this must be weighed the scope to spy, censor, control, manipulate, and otherwise suppress individuals, ideas and activities that may be seen as damaging or embarrassing to government. The temptation is that uncompetitive governments will at best, waste resources by unnecessary mass surveillance, and at worst, seek to employ technology to protect themselves, to mask their failure, to hide essential truths, to stifle debate, limit choice and competition itself.

The classic challenge is "quis custodiet ipsos custodes?" Well-resourced oversight is vitally important, for in the absence of adequate regulation and control, the benefits of competitive government itself can be undermined and the state weakened as a result. The risk is that without the right mechanisms in place, politicians will not even know, be told or understand, what an uncompetitive government is doing "to keep them and us safe" until it is too late to stop.

Ultimately, technology forces competitive government. The messages it sends, the choices it offers and the opportunities it presents champions and rewards good performance, just as it exposes and punishes bad. The use of technology requires and facilitates competitiveness. To be successful, government must focus on how it can best harness technology in all its forms to deliver maximum value. Technology on its own, however, does not guarantee the delivery of winning government. It is a tool rather than an end. Governments need to use competition to help them make the right decisions and judgments on policies and programs, and embrace technology to help them win.

THE NATURE OF COMPETITION

A competitive government is not only efficient and effective, but crucially, able to demonstrate its performance by comparison with other countries and internally within its borders. It is focused on citizen satisfaction – giving the best value to its people, in the same way that successful businesses concentrate on satisfying the wants of their customers. Competitive governments enhance opportunities, choices and life chances, helping citizens achieve their full potential and maximizing their happiness.

Competition comes in many forms, and in varying degrees of subtlety, all of which must be used to get the most benefit and the greatest value. It applies between countries but also within countries, and it is here that it is arguably an even more powerful force for improvement. It includes different agencies and layers of government competing with each other, private providers competing against government provision, together with near competitors doing similar functions to government, in the private sector. It covers policy decisions and delivery options, as well as program priorities and budget allocations.

Understanding how to engineer the benefits of competition into government, how to harness competitive forces, and how they can be used to improve performance is crucial to the delivery of competitive government. Competition helps to determine what government delivers and the way it should measure success. It is impossible to get the most out of competition unless there is clarity on objectives. Competition for what is the simple question? Competitive government requires, at the very least, a high level definition of what government is trying to accomplish. It stands at the pinnacle of the pyramid that can then be cascaded down to lower levels with greater substance and detail. Without this, competitive comparison can become meaningless. It is like attempting to assess performance in a race, minus a defined finishing line or any other objective to reach.

Identifying the mission of government should be simple and straight forward. Unfortunately, for many governments, it is not. Few governments succinctly define what they are aiming to achieve. If, when this book was written, you typed into Google something like "US Government Mission Statement," you would be disappointed with the results. This absence of lucidity undermines and impedes performance. While it may be difficult to articulate in detail, there can be no excuse for its glaring omission.

The supposition behind competitive government is that all governments have as their primary aim the generation of prosperity in its broadest sense. The desire to improve, to build on past achievements, to give children a better life than their parents, is fundamental to human existence. From this, objectives in all other areas flow. You cannot maximize prosperity if you lack, for instance, first class education or effective law enforcement. Governments have a duty of care to strive to deliver the best possible outcomes and the highest citizen satisfaction. It is in the nature of competition that the words vary, the emphasis is different, but the intention is the same. As nations and peoples want as much prosperity as they can achieve, the relative performance of government is vital to realizing that objective.

Competition between nations is the most visible form of competitive government. Countries can be compared and contrasted, with winners and losers emerging. Policies and programs can be examined, and their relative performance analyzed and assessed. Comparators can be relatively simple, the key feature is that they are meaningful and real. The important thing, however, is not to get too obsessed by the detail of specific measures, but to look at the broad picture that emerges.

Actual outcomes matter. Competitive government is not a statisticians' paradise, arguing over a percentage here, a ranking there, misses the point. The fundamental issue is whether a country is performing as well as it possibly could in generating prosperity for its citizens. How effectively does it use the assets of natural competitive advantage; such as physical resources, climate, geography, language, and how good it is at building additional national strengths and harnessing the skills of all? The proof of the pudding is in the eating. Success is self-evident, citizen satisfaction manifest. Countries with winning governments are judged as highly attractive places to live and invest now, and crucially, in the future. Even the most successful governments need to make sure that they avoid complacency, and are constantly looking for new ways of adding greater value.

Governments that perform less well in the competitive challenge face questions such as why, and more importantly, how can they improve? Responses can be superficial or fundamental. Countries, will probably use a mixture of the two, however it is only the second that offers long term success. Enduring prosperity is only secured if it has foundations built on rock. Nations that fail to make their governments and societies truly competitive, are eclipsed by others more willing to change. For instance, virtually every government seeks to compete for business investment through a combination of grants, subsidies, reliefs and other indulgences. Thus multinational corporations or high profile projects are induced to locate in one country versus another. This sort of phony competition between countries fronts the news, and is normally presented in terms of a government success, creating countless jobs and opportunities.

What fails to command the headlines, however, is the far larger number of jobs lost or not created by indigenous corporations because of unfriendly government taxes and regulations, and poor public services. Indeed, it is perverse that governments try to claim credit for getting round the consequences of their own policies. Even more telling is that they have to do so in the first place. Beggar thy neighbor competition does nothing to address the issues that dog a country's performance, the winning of investment from a multinational is a mere pinprick as far as overall national prosperity is concerned.

The obverse of trying to attract businesses is striving to stop them leaving by imposing measures that frustrate normal commercial decisions. Attempts at this type of anti-competition can be buttressed with international treaties, and may be hedged with reassuring words such as seeking to crack down on tax avoidance and promoting harmonization. Effort is lavished upon such fruitless endeavors instead of working to make a government more competitive. Governments who think they can increase the prosperity of their people by building artificial barriers are gravely mistaken. Rather than seeking to prevent existing wealth fleeing, they must concentrate on creating the best environment for its generation. The most successful countries are those that focus ruthlessly on the development of policies and programs for business growth, and free trade.

Fundamental competition concerns increasing the value added of government activity, and how successful government is in leveraging high quality outcomes. Really competitive countries have first class education, health care and infrastructure; they are secure and safe places to do business, with a tax, regulatory and legal system that fosters success. Governments that aim to be competitive have to ask questions such as, how does taxing corporations help them perform better? Does this levy on employment encourage the creation of jobs or deter it? Does this regulation make it less likely or more likely that successful products and services will be developed?

As businesses, and increasingly people, become more mobile, the attractions of locating and expanding in countries with competitive governments grows ever greater. Of course, it would be wrong to over dramatize this observation; every business would not leave, but the quality of government is a major factor in investment decisions and commercial success. Uncompetitive government means that even the most competitive businesses are disadvantaged, compared to those operating in a country with a better performing government.

Success in fundamental competition is a developing trend, mirroring the progress of government competitiveness. No government can hope to be excellent in all areas, but slowly almost imperceptibly, competitive governments attract more businesses and more talented people. The result is a virtuous cycle of increased prosperity that translates into still greater competitiveness. Those governments that are laggardly find themselves subject to a vicious spiral that makes them even less competitive. Without facilitating new successful businesses and with overburdened existing ones; the combination of higher taxes, more borrowing and poorer public services leads to further decline.

A government can only be internationally competitive if it understands, embraces and responds to the competitive pressures within its own country. Competition is not only for what it does, but how it is delivered and how responsive it is to customer demand. Governments face internal competition in a number of ways. Direct competition encompasses those providing the same or very similar services, indirect includes doing work that is akin to government functions. For instance, in areas such as law enforcement it is in competition with criminals, and in taxation, it faces evasion and avoidance. Frequently it can face competition as a consequence of its own failure to deliver, with private schools, hospitals and security firms stepping in to make good. To get the most from this competition, government needs to appreciate the true nature of its own services, what is actually being provided, and what it really costs. Evaluating its performance, understanding how it can do better, learning from others, is vital to improve the value of overall provision.

Government can also be in competition with itself. This can happen between different departments and agencies essentially trying to do the same thing. Turf wars and overlapping activities can be extremely wasteful, sowing confusion over responsibilities and outcomes. While removing unintended rivalry is important for efficiency, at the same time it is vital to recognize that there are many ways of skinning a cat, and an element of internal competition can help provide the best services. Few functions are completely standalone, managing interdependences and cross cutting initiatives can yield greater competitive benefits than traditional structures and hierarchies.

Competitive governments are extremely aware of the unintended consequences of past and future policies. Few, for instance, set out to greatly expand the accountancy or legal professions, yet complex tax laws, or a climate that encourages litigation, achieve precisely this outcome. Observing market signals, and seeing them as a cue for measures such as tax simplification cuts the need for both tax inspectors and professional advisers, creating a competitive win-win.

Government is in competition with technology, as innovation challenges existing ways of delivery and working practices. While some might like to continue government activities unchanged and oblivious to progress, new opportunities mean that it has to respond, or be seen as increasingly out of touch and remote. By way of a small example, public libraries provide a case study on how it must adapt to new realities.

Facilitating competition within the government hierarchy, crafting its structure to promote the provision of services in a way most likely to benefit from the application of competitive forces, is essential. Here the principle of subsidiarity is key. Challenges should be dealt with at the level most appropriate for their effective solution. Encouraging the devolution of powers back to cities and local regions, away from federal or central government is a vital step in the process. In local government, competitive comparison is very helpful at understanding relative performance, and highlighting best practice. Such measures go hand in hand with making local government itself more competitive and competent, developing the concept of the enterprising municipality or council, working in partnership with, and adding value, to communities. While relaxing control increases the risks of "failure", it is easily outweighed by the wider benefits of success.

Competitive government is also in competition for good people, not just to run its services but to boost national performance. As well as creating an education system that gets the most from its own citizens, winning governments headhunt from other countries. In addition to attracting people to come of their own volition, positive immigration policies seek out talent and skills, rather as corporations recruit their employees.

Competition is often seen extremely negatively by those working within the public sector, and the unions who represent them. Instead of the route to deliver better services, greater value and more rewarding employment opportunities, it is associated with job cuts and deteriorating standards. As a result, there is a tendency to stifle competition, instead of using it to improve provision. Processes such as competitive tendering are usually handled poorly, reinforcing resistance. For competitive government to succeed there is a need to counter the view that government is like an Ameglian cow waiting to be carved up and devoured by predators. Partly this is the result of a failure to communicate the vision of what government is there to achieve, partly it is a lack of faith that government, and those who work for it, can be successful in delivering high quality services that add real value to their countries and societies. Competition needs to be appreciated as freeing public employees to show how good they really are, rather than exposing how badly they are performing. Employees must be listened to and actively involved – as those closest to service provision, they often have the best ideas on how it can be improved. Unions have a vital role to play, acting in the best interests of their members, working in a progressive partnership to remove the barriers to improvement instead of threatening destructive confrontation in the face of change. Conversely, where union representatives are 'in bed' with underperforming managers, the cozy relationships should be dissolved as this also gets in the way of progress.

Adopting the concept of enterprising government is a key feature of the competitive process. It is one that takes risks, that innovates, that uses competition as a creative force to ensure that government gets most from its assets and abilities. Government must compete to deliver best value outcomes, if it is successful it expands, if it fails, it contracts. Competition helps drive efficiency, it requires the identification and definition of products and services, the ability to properly cost and price what is offered and engage in a comprehensive evaluation of performance. Such an approach harnesses the skills of staff, and motivates rather than alienates them. Giving those providing services commercial freedoms, cutting away layers of superfluous management, and imposing business-like disciplines and rewards, are vital to get the most from government employees.

Of course competition is also present between different policies and programs. While the battle over the allocation of budgets is a traditional skirmish, securing and using competitive information on the efficacy of relative outcomes can fundamentally change the nature of the debate.

There are no "no-go" areas for competitive government, although the way competition is handled and managed is different, depending on the scope of the activity. Certain services, it is sometimes argued, are too important to be exposed to competition or are natural monopolies where competition would be senseless and wasteful. Starting with this approach is like looking through the wrong end of a telescope. Food is a vital human need, yet how many governments seek to produce, distribute and sell food? Agricultural policies are one thing, but overwhelmingly food is provided by competitive suppliers giving a broad range of choice. It is true that it would be nonsensical to have rival water pipes or sewerage services in a street, but that does not stop competitive pressures being applied to drive up performance. In virtually every area opportunities exist to use competition or contestability to secure better value, whether this be changing the nature of services, how they are supplied or the extent to which back office functions are shared. Effective regulation that builds on and develops best practice, is an essential service that competitive governments provide.

There is no such thing as perfect competition; competitive government is not about theory but reality. Obviously areas such as national security have to be treated differently to garbage collection. Issues such as ownership, accountability and loyalty matter. It would be no good having your enemy putting in a low bid to provide your defense and winning the contract. Competitive governments focus on ensuring they have the most effective defense, while getting rid of elements that are no longer relevant or essential to the mission. They ensure that they use competition wisely to best deliver their objectives. Within the military, for instance, at the highest level competition exists in evaluating potential enemies and how other countries address similar challenges. It is present when considering options for dealing with threats, increasingly these can be addressed through nonphysical measures, which can totally change the dynamics of the response. The idea of winning without fighting has been at the heart of diplomatic maneuvering for centuries, and it is something winning governments seek to deliver. Lower down the ladder, there is competition between different arms and corps, it exists between rival suppliers, weapon systems and technology.

For those who are still skeptical, the unescapable reality is that for everything government does, competition can be applied in one form or another, and that the benefits of the process easily outweigh its costs. Indeed, the costs of failing to use competition are considerably greater although these may not be readily apparent. Competition fosters innovation; functions that are subject to active competitive forces are far more likely to develop efficient ways of carrying out tasks than those sheltered from its pressures. Competition encourages accountability and transparency, it rewards success and punishes failure. It is in the nature of competitive government that those most affected by the outcomes judge the results. There is no place for a poorly performing public organization in a country with a winning government. It simply should not exist. That does not mean that current staff will be out of work, but that they are employed contributing to the generation of wealth and prosperity elsewhere.

Competitive governments use competition in all its forms to attain success. They promote and reinforce the power of choice in every aspect of their operation, seeing it as the oil lubricating the machinery of the State. They help citizens access choice, giving capacity and the ability to navigate options. They upscale winners and cut losers. More competitive governments deliver better value for money than less competitive ones. Given the importance of government, it is axiomatic that those states that are more prosperous are more likely to possess a winning government than those languishing in relative economic decline.

DELIVERING WINNING GOVERNMENT

Winning government is the antithesis of losing government. To deliver, countries must first confront the reality of what leads or has led their government to be uncompetitive, and then go further, harnessing competition to ensure their government's administration and programs are rooted in excellence and best practice. In looking at the problems, it is evident that inconvenient truths lie behind many of the observations. As government improves the relevance of the analysis diminishes but this increases its value as a guard against regression and recidivism. It is worth noting that not all the challenges are evident in all countries, and that some vary in degree, but that all governments are capable of improvement. There can be no absolute model of what is necessary to deliver a winning government. By its nature it consists of a large variety of components, themselves changing and evolving to meet new circumstances and challenges. It is possible, however, to define certain characteristics that point to success.

Winning governments know what they want to achieve, with a clear hierarchy of priorities, and a very good understanding of how they interrelate. They are responsive and dynamic, enterprising and entrepreneurial, with a strong drive to succeed. They listen to their citizens, and be constantly striving to give improved products and services that are consistently more efficacious. They research and evaluate new approaches to problems, facilitating choices, seeking out best practice and identifying relative underperformance; continually looking to replace less effective policies and programs with better ones. Crucial is the notion of adding value. They do not provide a service where someone else can offer better value.

Winning governments pay their own way. They do not have structural deficits and borrow to finance current expenditure. They aim not only for a balanced budget but to generate surpluses that can be used to finance investment, and to provide for shortfalls in funding due to economic downturns. Consistent "profits" rather than endemic "losses" are the key to sustainable government competitiveness.

For winning government to be delivered, three elements must be put in place. Each is mutually supportive, and it is hard to envisage success without all three.

First, winning government needs public support, in the absence of this progress is virtually impossible. The toleration of failing government is driven by ignorance, impotence and apathy. Competitive government contends that as the failures of losing government become more and more visible, popular sentiment will demand change and elect politicians to deliver it. Faced with the knowledge of relative failure, and the choice of improvement, it is inconceivable that voters will choose to stick with an uncompetitive government indefinitely. Creating the environment for winning government is a bit like addressing the conundrum of what comes first, the chicken or the egg? For the purpose of analysis and reflecting the nature of democracy, the issues are examined in the order of citizens driving politicians, driving government to change. It does not have to happen in this way. It is possible that a highly charismatic and determined politician can lead change, and secure a popular mandate by articulating the importance of winning government before voters appreciate it themselves.

Second, the machinery of government must be fundamentally

overhauled not only to make it competitive, but agile, enterprising and capable of sustaining winning policies. In particular, the will to win, to deliver the best, should be at the heart of the ethos of public service. The old adage that it is not coming first that matters, it is the taking part, may serve as consolation to those who do not succeed, but in reality, very few can sustain what it takes to be competitive without the passion to excel. There needs to be a realization that the passive acceptance of underperformance is corrupt; that the duty of those in public office is to always seek excellence and that second best, or worse, is simply unacceptable.

Third, winning governments ensure that all their policies and programs are geared to the achievement of their objectives. Policies must recognize success, and allow resources to be redeployed or released so that they can then be employed in relatively higher value activities. Implicit is a judgment about increasing or lowering taxes. Governments tax more if they can offer greater value, but they cut taxes, if leaving money with citizens or corporations gives greater benefit. Winning policies and programs are examined in detail in the next chapter.

Winning public support

Securing popular support is crucial for the delivery of winning government. This is both easy and hard.

In countries with uncompetitive governments, citizen dissatisfaction with the evolution of government is manifest. Countless opinion polls and surveys show that people lack confidence in the ability of government to address the problems they face. Citizens regard government as unfriendly, unproductive, unsuccessful and wasteful. Words such as efficient and responsive are hardly ever associated with the public sector. Large numbers believe that a significant proportion of government outlays are squandered. In comparison with their own activities or those of corporations, citizens rarely value the contribution of government to their own well-being. These perceptions are often reinforced not only by day-to-day experiences of dealing with public bodies, but also through seemingly endless official reports condemning poor performance and mismanagement by government agencies.

People no longer believe that government does the right thing, and acts in their best interests. Government is ceasing to be a creative force, but is becoming more of a burden or an obstacle to be circumvented. It is seen as distant; it fails to deal with real problems in a sensible way. Instead of appreciating the citizen's desire for speed, simplicity and efficiency, virtually every transaction is at some stage or another characterized with delay, frustration and obtuseness.

This disillusionment can translate into lamentable turnouts at elections, street protests, and dalliance with extremists. There is a general contempt for mainstream politicians, an antipathy reinforced by accounts of sleaze and corruption, a view that people are only in public life for what they can get out of it; that serving the public is a distant, and often forgotten, motive for seeking office. Politicians have lost trust, become detached from the struggles of everyday existence, the battle to pay for necessities, to make ends meet from one paycheck to the next.

Given this degree of cynicism, it may seem strange that popular sentiment is by far the hardest area to motivate. There needs to be a transition away from a passive dissatisfaction with government, and a reluctance to acquiesce to higher taxes, to positive action to do something about it. Experience shows that people are remarkably ambivalent and tolerant toward government. There is a level of resignation that is much greater than would be expected if a corporation or store were too expensive and delivering poor quality products. Undoubtedly, this is self-serving, it has much to do with the perception of government as a monopoly with citizens having no choice, being forced to pay taxes and accept its services. If there is nothing that can be done, why bother trying? People get on with their own lives, seek to maximize their happiness the best they can, and devote little thought to improving government.

Government itself can nurture this impotence, indeed it feeds it, stoking fear of change. In age-old fashion, and helped by the fact that more, and more, have become at least partially dependent on government, radical change is linked with people "losing" benefits, entitlements, jobs, pensions, and services. It is human nature to hope for the best, to want unfunded promises to be true, and to believe that things will turn out alright in the end. Why risk rocking the boat? Better the devil you know; things could be much worse.

The fundamental problem, however, is that the reality of underperformance makes it harder and harder to sustain an uncompetitive government. As technology changes, as new products and services evolve, these are likely to require even greater resources; a country with a losing government struggles and ultimately fail to provide them. With progress the cake grows, and the slices get proportionately bigger. Countries that don't grow the cake, find themselves unable to match the services delivered by those with a winning government. Borrowing and bailing out by neighbors only delays the inevitable, and makes it worse. The challenge for the defenders of uncompetitive government is that failing to respond to popular feeling and resentment does not make it go away. Instead it simmers and festers, looking for an opportunity, waiting for the moment to be tapped or released.

Competitive government elsewhere hastens this process. As citizens become more aware of the relative under performance of their government, they demand improvement and better choices. Questions start; "why are people in that country more prosperous, why do they have better schools, why can't I get better health care, why do I have to pay higher taxes, why am I a victim of crime, why is the economy going downhill, why can't my children get jobs?" and so on. Gradually the idea that tolerating underperformance is somehow acceptable becomes increasingly alien to citizens, politicians and public employees alike. Spurred on by their personal experience and ultimately propelled by forces that they cannot control, those who work in government have to respond. Either they make their government more competitive, or they face national bankruptcy, followed by competitive government. Competitive government comes, there is no sustainable alternative.

The transition from complacency to competency, the adoption of competitive government will be shorter in some countries than in others, but ultimately irresistible for all. Success requires a re-engagement in the political process, with people seeing politics as the chance to make a material difference to their lives, and one in which they need to take an active part. That change can be fast tracked, encouraged and nurtured is undeniable; the benefits of embracing competitive government voluntarily, rather than being coerced, are immeasurably great, but this challenge is down to a country's politicians.

The delivery of winning government requires courage. Countries may be fortunate in finding the right leaders before the problems become too large. For the process to start it needs such an individual in a major country to pick up the gauntlet, and all other countries will be compelled to follow suit. Once people have experienced the benefits of competitive government, it is inconceivable that they will want to regress. By definition, uncompetitive government does not have the leaders it needs to change. The political system has failed to respond to the challenges that the development of government has created. Countries face the dilemma of the increasing complexity of government, at a time when the general quality of politicians, and their leadership abilities, is declining. Most politicians pose little threat to uncompetitive government. Indeed, to be selected to represent one of the "ruling parties" they have undoubtedly expressed views that espouse radicalism in favor of the status quo. Real choices are not offered, political debate tends to be focused on the margins of government activity, a spending decision here, a relatively small tax cut there, all pepped up with petty point scoring over who is to blame, and ideally flavored with a juicy scandal involving one or more of the candidates for office. All of this is supported by a news media that is frequently far too close to the government, and the ruling establishment to challenge the prevailing orthodoxy.

Legislatures came into existence to stop, or at least constrain, the executive from spending taxpayer dollars unwisely. Now not only have the legislators changed their spots, and are principally concerned with spending money, their ability to check and hold administrations to account has been severely curtailed by the growth of government. Instead of scrutiny, the tendency, when not gridlocked by political maneuvering, is to fuel the expansion, introducing new programs and passing ever more laws and regulations to be policed.

How often do you hear the offhand remark that such a president or prime minister is "running the country"? The truth is far from the case. In fact, their ability to take control and make even minor changes is extremely limited. The nature of the political system and the structure of government, with its checks and balances, coupled with the weight of decades of bureaucracy, has made it much harder for leaders to have a dramatic impact. The short termism of political life, and the dominance of the electoral timescale mean that as issues become more complex and action more difficult, politicians lose interest in wholesale reform, preferring palliative instead of radical change. Due to the sheer scale of government, it is hardly surprising that politicians have problems in efficiently managing such a massive undertaking. When compared to the private sector, very few businesses get close to the size of even a small government, and those multinationals that do, have senior managers and executives that are steeped in layers of business qualifications, corporate training and with years of expertise. Yet, quite often, the person "running the country" and those who support him or her, have virtually no inkling of what it takes to run a large organization, or even a corner store. Many are lawyers, journalists and academics instead of managers, they have normally climbed up the lower rungs of office or party infrastructure, rather than had real business experience. Even in republics, a near hereditary system can take root where children succeed parents, spouse follows spouse, as "ruling" families take control.

Uncompetitive government is dogged by the creation of a political class that seeks office for its own sake. It is schooled in the arts of getting into government, climbing the greasy pole, but not in managing it once elected. As a result, it is seldom that those who are best able to govern are in the positions of political power. The problem is that it has become virtually impossible to attract the finest into politics. Competitive pressures elsewhere mean that for the good people government needs, other career options are just too enticing. The delivery of winning government requires exceptional talent, with experience and drive. Making politics appeal to these people demands a fundamental change, tackling the obstacles to their recruitment. It applies not only to the president or prime minister, but for all elected positions.

Government should compete much more effectively for its political leaders. The first and most obvious way to secure better individuals, is to reward them appropriately. Creating genuine competition for public office requires salaries and rewards, which reflect the nature of the responsibilities politicians are required to take on, and to compensate them for the pressures and constraints of the democratic system. It is reasonable to expect a president or prime minister to attract a package at least on a par with the average of the country's top ten CEO's. Salaries for lower level positions should be set accordingly. The political process should be independently and fairly funded, and candidates who are unsuccessful in being elected should be recompensed for running for public office. Those who baulk at such proposals, need to think long and hard about the alternatives. In this context, the saying that "if you pay peanuts, you get monkeys," has a particular resonance. The overall increase in cost, of course, is mitigated countless times over by the delivery of winning government. Cutting the number of political posts, especially the size of legislatures, makes it considerably easier to find enough competent people, and reduces the scope for idle hands in congress or parliament performing the devil's work. It is not only about money, however, the underlying hope is that countries with uncompetitive governments are fortunate to discover leaders who are motivated by a far greater calling than just financial reward.

The second way, and ultimately more important, is to create an environment in which it is possible to get things done. Politics under competitive government is far more about levels of competence than prejudice and conviction. It centers not on what politicians think, in theory, might work, but rather on what actually does deliver and the pursuit and development of proven best practice. The realization of winning government would raise the status and stature of politicians immeasurably. So success requires not only outstanding political leadership, but a new government machine that gives effective control and management over the delivery of policies and programs, within a devolved and competitive framework.

Enterprising government

Winning governments need an infrastructure that is capable of securing policy objectives in a way that maximizes government's contribution to national prosperity. Stimulating enterprising government is about reasserting control and accountability, creating an organization that is entrepreneurial, that has a bias for action, which actually works, and can be managed successfully to deliver real value. A key part of this is addressing the nature of public service, making fundamental changes in the culture and operation of public employees. In this context, understanding what has gone wrong with government is central to putting it right. Pondering the quip about the nine most terrifying words in the English language being: "I'm from the government and I'm here to help," highlights the problem. The statement should not be a joke. The fact is that government should be there to promote, not hinder success.

The reality is that uncompetitive government has got bogged down, and is failing to deliver. In many fields, governments have expanded beyond their own competence, and cannot cope with the new demands and changed circumstances of the present day. Despite increased prosperity and dramatic advances in most areas of human endeavor, the capacity of government to deal with problems seems to be diminishing. More often than not, the immediate response of politicians to failure has been to introduce more programs and increase expenditure. If there is an issue, it is one of lack of resources, one which could be cured if only people would pay a little more and dig a little deeper. Instead of concentrating on succeeding at the original task, government has typically sought to address incompetence by expanding its provision elsewhere. Behaving almost like a child, it becomes bored with what it is doing; frustrated, it loses interest, and moves on, starting a new activity without finishing the first.

As government has grown, agencies have been set up in

response to a need or to solve an issue. Often the underlying problem slowly passes away but the agencies remain. Governments have departments "for" such and such, very rarely do they actually deal effectively with the challenges faced. Initial responsibilities are broadened, new roles established without any proper understanding of the impact on existing policies or activities. Each seems sensible on its own, but collectively government becomes a mess. Over time, a panoply of uncoordinated measures and programs emerges, fragmenting and fracturing resources. Complexity undermines efficiency, but it reinforces the status quo. The more involved the interaction between subsidies and tax breaks, the trickier it is to address issues through radical change. The web of cross cutting programs increase administrative burdens, confuse beneficiaries, waste taxpayers money and limit overall effectiveness. Frequently it is not clear whether programs are succeeding or failing in meeting their objectives. Where evidence is visible, attributing praise or blame is problematical, making it harder to favor one initiative and down grade another.

In this environment, even when success is identified, government fails to recognize its achievement by shutting down a program, and so is unable to release resources to address new challenges. Government finds it tough to change and continues applying outdated policies and programs to problems that have evolved, and thereby gradually becomes less effective at achieving the desired results. While it is relatively easy to build on a green field site, it is something else to demolish existing infrastructures and rebuild. The old crowds out the new.

This inflexibility is buttressed by the growth of powerful lobby groups. Once a program is established, very quickly its recipients organize to support it. Those who benefit directly from expenditure, effectively use some of the help they receive, to fund lobbying activities to protect their funding, and to secure further assistance. Politicians find themselves trapped by initiatives they put in place. This, in turn, can hinder further experimentation and innovation. Not all policies succeed, but knowing that it is virtually impossible to stop measures once they are started, means that ideas can be still born, the price of failure being too high. A similar situation exists with pork barrel funding. Once programs and projects have been widely distributed amongst politicians' constituencies, it is very hard to secure change. The losers from cuts seem immediate, translating into lost votes; the winners from doing something else with the resource, more remote. To govern is to choose, but it is much easier for politicians and officials to avoid difficult decisions. Yet it is precisely in this reluctance to decide that government is failing to do its duty.

Judgment is frustrated in any case, for losing government often operates bereft of useful information on its relative performance. Deficiencies exist because government believes it is different, its priorities are not those of efficiency and effectiveness that guide other enterprises, however the lack of the profit motive means it requires more data not less. Instead comfort is drawn from the vagaries of the political cycle, the presumption that secretaries or ministers are really not that interested in the boring day-to-day detail of operations, so it is not something that senior officials need to worry too much about either.

Losing government lacks the language of competition. In order for a business to compete successfully, it is crucial for it to understand its performance, and then manage actively to improve it. Such improvements rarely happen by accident or through omission. In government, the dearth of proper management and financial information undermines any assessment of progress. Departments and agencies try to hide behind the contention that it is impossible to properly measure what they do, so therefore, they do not see much point in trying. While this may be true for a small amount of government activity, for the vast majority of its programs it is plain nonsense. However, it is extremely rare that agencies make any attempt to define, cost and assess performance based on their outputs or outcomes.

Even when they do, there is often little understanding of how the outputs contribute to successful delivery of outcomes. This cuts both ways, for although ignorance on the costs of outputs and outcomes frees officials from accountability in the short term, it undermines potentially good arguments for increasing budgets. If agencies could show conclusively the impact of additional funding on improving performance, then it may be easier to provide more resources, switch priorities and ask voters to pay higher taxes to get greater value.

In fact, most budgets are seldom allocated on any more sensible basis than what the body spent last year plus a certain percentage for inflation, minus any deemed efficiency saving. Where significant sums are committed to new projects, it is frequently without any real understanding of how the investment changes or improves the current service. Business cases are produced, but the culture is such that rarely are these projects properly costed, partly because of the lack of wider financial data from existing operations. The temptation is to make projects appear cheaper than they actually are, with the cynical intention of securing additional funding once the initiative has acquired a momentum that makes it financially or politically impossible to stop. As costs rise, the claimed benefits usually diminish. While departments are good at spending money they are far less proficient when it comes to realizing the fruits of their investment.

Most departmental and agency budgets are input rather than output focused. They concentrate on account code items, such as salaries and wages, travel expenses, purchases of services and commodities, instead of planning what outcome is to be delivered, establishing a competitive cost and working backwards to come up with a budget requirement. Scrutiny of budgets is limited with there being an almost inverse relationship to the amount of funding concerned. Attention can be lavished on relatively trifling sums for travel or refreshments at meetings, but expenditures of millions or even tens of millions are nodded through. Typically, those in charge of "getting value for money" can relate to and challenge issues such as the quality or quantity of cookies, whereas they have precious little understanding of the merits or otherwise of larger expenditure. Thus savings of $1,000 may be squeezed from planned expenditure on snacks and success is achieved; the scrutinizers have done their work, and potentially millions is wasted elsewhere.

In year financial management is of the most basic level and across the world trillions of dollars are spent according to processes that are little better than those employed with a child's piggy bank. Bodies operate on a "spend it or lose it" principle, whereby if they do not consume all their funding by the end of the fiscal year they not only get the money taken from them, but, like as not, receive a reduced amount the following year. Hence you have the unseemly and extremely wasteful practice of agencies splurging significant amounts of their budgets in the last three months of the financial year. Often this develops into a feeding frenzy for suppliers. Rarely is value for money obtained through this lack of financial control and planning. At least the child gets to keep what it has not spent.

Unlike competitive corporations, very few governments make any use of sensible accounting procedures, employing instead simple cash-based systems. Resource or accruals accounting is standard practice for businesses across the developed world. Without it you cannot run, and manage a successful, competitive enterprise. For government amongst other things it would highlight the relationship between its capital and current expenditure, spotlight vast estates of underperforming assets, and draw attention to their massive liabilities established over time. Due to the inadequacies of the accounting systems, managers seldom receive accurate and timely reports during the course of the year. Often they are required to spend blindly, or even keep their own set of books. In any one department there could be a number of different accounting systems. Across a government there may be hundreds, this fragmentation does not permit the consolidation of data to provide useful information on the true costs of achieving outcomes.

It is hardly surprising, therefore, that not many public bodies could pass any type of normal commercial audit, and can even find their accounts qualified by much laxer government standards. Rarely is this financial mess acknowledged or treated with the seriousness it deserves, thus little is actually done to improve the situation. Yet without proper financial and performance information, it is virtually impossible for the executive, legislatures and ultimately the citizen to properly hold government to account. Government cannot be competitive if it lacks the ability to understand and control its finances in a fashion that permit comparison and evaluation.

The creation of a winning government requires and demands fundamental change. First, in most countries, a wholesale restructuring of government is needed to ensure that its organization is geared to the most efficient and effective delivery of outcomes. The problems with government bureaucracies are so ingrained that probably it is cleaner and easier to start a fresh, rather than seek to modify what currently exists. A transformational not incremental process is required. The transition from A to B is harder in some nations than others, but in conception it is relatively easy. Starting with a blank sheet it is straight-forward to sketch out the key priorities, and design a structure to be responsible for their delivery. Its focus is different from traditional approaches, far more flexible than established departmental silos, embracing a new mind set with an emphasis on collaborative working across many disciplines. Instead of comprising a large number of departments and agencies, government concentrate on pooling effort, joining up services to make them citizen friendly and leveraging resources to get the highest value outcomes. At the heart of the framework is a clear understanding of the need for government to maximize its contribution to the creation of prosperity and national competitiveness.

As part of this evaluation, appreciating the scope for

international collaboration in improving competitiveness is essential. For smaller countries in areas such as foreign policy and defense, working with others through multinational structures can not only enhance effectiveness but reduce cost. Bigger countries can get similar advantages from trade and customs unions. The need is to realize the benefits from membership of international organizations, frequently the tendency is to sign up, but then to keep the relatively ineffective national government functions largely unchanged, effectively duplicating rather than rationalizing resources.

The structure of competitive government is very similar across countries. In essence, it is geared to encouraging, harnessing and incentivizing competition and choice at all levels of government, and from all sources. It concentrates on listening to citizens, promoting what works, and getting rid of what does not. It seeks new ways of delivery, including making the most appropriate use of technology to deliver the best solutions.

Second, competitive governments manage in the same way as successful corporations. They need a "business plan" that links outcomes with financial and performance data. The figures are put together in accordance with commercial accounting practice. They establish a work program that embraces all the activities of government, starting with the most important. It covers how improvements in performance will be delivered over a period of years, highlighting the benefits of investments and responses to competitive pressures. It contains properly costed outcomes and outputs to facilitate competitive comparison. A key feature of the approach is transparency. It focuses attention on the value delivered by the big ticket items that consume most of government resources. It assists in identifying areas where government can offer greater value, and is falling behind its competitors. The work program is also a vital tool to help administrations measure citizen satisfaction, prioritize, take informed decisions and be held accountable for results. Information on performance is especially useful when it comes to axing or curtailing old programs in favor of new ones. The whole process gives politicians and the public a much better understanding of what government does, the value it adds and how it might be improved.

Effective management requires strong financial controls and comprehensive reporting of performance. This is essential to avoid waste, and to maximize the use of resources to deliver the best value. Much greater professionalism will be demonstrated in the letting, evaluation and management of contracts. Competitive businesses succeed in managing complex networks of sub-contractors and other suppliers, and competitive governments should do the same. Government must ensure that services are procured in the right way, with payments linked to the successful achievement of outcomes. Securing best value is about far more than just accepting the cheapest tender, it includes building in flexibility, encouraging innovation and the sharing of risk. Governments need to guard against being trapped in situations where they cannot go elsewhere, a central element of getting the most from competition is to encourage new entrants, to preserve contestability, and give choice over future providers.

What emerges is a government that is dynamic and enterprising, easier to control and hold accountable for its results. At its heart a small core of highly competent directors and managers, overseeing a much larger workforce in arm's length organizations, actually delivering public services alongside corporations, and not-for-profit groups. The focus is on managing the efficient delivery of policies and programs, and undertaking competitive analysis of how outcomes could be improved. Evident difficulties exist in establishing really autonomous organizations within government, although many countries have already gone a significant way down this route. The vital aspect is giving such bodies the freedom to compete, allowing them to expand or contract depending on their performance. The challenge should not be allowed to frustrate the initiative, rather embolden leadership and spur action.

Third, winning governments innovate, taking risks in order to succeed. It involves strategic thinking about satisfying future needs and developing practical solutions, in addition to coming up with ways in which existing services can be delivered better. It is about investing in research and development, creating new markets for businesses to satisfy. Using taxpayer dollars to leverage the potential of transformative technologies, placing bets that would not be commercially attractive is a vital leadership role that only governments can perform. Building on the shoulders of giants, empowering government to stimulate national success, demands the right skills and competences are present in public service, as well as a more relaxed view of failure, and the ability to learn from mistakes. Indeed, accepting and recognizing failure is at the heart of the competitive process.

None of this is rocket science, it reflects what successful businesses do every day, builds on decades of experience and models taught in business schools around the world, and is used by major corporations at one extreme and start-ups at the other. While straight forward, the implementation and delivery presents the ultimate test, for it requires a revolution as far as many public employees in losing governments are concerned.

Excellent people

Winning government has excellent people; outstanding management talent, with highly motivated staff doing real jobs, that clearly contribute to the realization of key priorities. Uncompetitive government is characterized by poor management, overstaffing and low morale. It is crucial here to draw a distinction between the "bosses" and the "workers". Millions of people work for government doing vital tasks, most will still be employed, with increases in the areas that add most value. The argument is that these workers are frequently let down by weak leadership and the way government has evolved. Making government competitive frees them to do their jobs better. To improve, public service must recruit, train and promote senior managers in the same fashion as successful corporations.

Instead, losing government all too frequently prizes non-management qualities such as the ability to draft papers, argue points and avoid risk, to balance all the arguments, to only make a decision in extremis; theoretical values rather than practical knowledge, and even the capacity of a candidate to contribute toward a quota target. Application procedures are long and involved, characterized by inflexibility and lack of imagination. Once recruited, promotion, although usually on merit, is merit judged by the standards of the organization. Unlike in the commercial world, where the competitive pressure to succeed drives advancement and selection, the public service career ladder becomes increasingly incestuous. As senior officials are rarely managers they tend not to promote managers, but favor people in their own image. Those who challenge the status quo, have new ideas, are innovative and competent, are often actively discouraged. They do not get promoted, or it is on a slower track, and they fall behind their more compliant colleagues. The failure to recognize and reward talented managers is a fundamental problem. Invariably good people within government become frustrated and resign. Some find leaving is not a simple option due to the stigma of working for uncompetitive government, so they fester, becoming cynical of those promoted above them, demotivated they may obstruct change, either deliberately or by omission.

In many countries, the civil service is characterized by the cult of the generalist, perhaps better described as the well-intentioned amateur. The obverse is the cult of the technocrat, someone who is so steeped in the "arts" of public service that business-like management is an anathema bordering on heresy. Like all government employees, they are hide bound with rules and regulations. Civil service codes may guard against corruption with a capital "C" but unwittingly support corruption with a small "c", being permissive of waste, inefficiency, unresponsiveness and poor value for money. Frequently, it is not so much what is actually lost, it is the potential opportunities forgone that is most disastrous for good government. The consequence is that over time uncompetitive government has been saddled with layers of bureaucracy that get in the way of action. Not only are there far too many managers, increasingly, monitoring has supplanted managing. Rather than leading and encouraging workers to display initiative, managers start to knit pick over minutiae or withdraw into just answering emails and going to meetings – indeed most "managers" have little idea how to manage in the first place. In this environment it is understandable that employees lose any drive they might possess, sit back, keep their heads down and coast along, anticipating early retirement and the receipt of their generous inflation-proofed pensions divorced from the realities of government's performance.

Occasional attempts to bring in experience from outside are usually half-hearted at best, and seldom yield any significant improvement. Here salary, status and the way government functions undermines the initiative. In the spirit of open competition advertisements are placed for agency executives, finance directors and other senior positions. Yet, when the package on offer is examined, normally dictated by salaries elsewhere in government, it is pitched at a level that is unlikely to attract the top caliber skills government needs. Not only would a suitable individual have to take a pay cut possibly running into hundreds of thousands of dollars, they could lose stock options and other perks. Even if they were prepared to make the sacrifice, they would have to adapt to government's old fashioned ways of working, for instance accounting that is nothing like proper accounting, and human resource practices that are stuck in a government time warp. On taking the job, they would become islands of business-like sense surrounded by a sea of blurry public sector ethos. Not only would they talk a different language, they would always be seen as an outsider – "not one of us" – a token rather than somebody who has a real role to play. They lack the support mechanisms upon which they had relied, and find it extremely hard to have a significant impact. Those who attempt to shake things up find themselves hamstrung by political constraints and bureaucratic handcuffs. Few trouble shooters would operate successfully if they could not change how people worked, drop unsuccessful programs and projects, close offices and free up resources for new investment. The result is that nine times out of ten, those recruited from the private sector are second or third tier talent, perhaps passed over, or near retirement. It is hardly surprising that they fail to display the dynamism that government needs to improve. All this reinforces the prejudice in government, that it has very little to learn from elsewhere.

Likewise, the direct recruitment of experienced outsiders for middle or junior management positions is very limited. Here, even if the selection process is not "fixed" as is customary for internal posts, instead of appointing people who could contribute more to the organization, there is a strong bias to avoid bringing in those who could be seen as a threat to the established orthodoxy, or might challenge the lack of competence of existing managers and aspire to their jobs.

In losing governments there is a failure to manage human resources at anything more advanced than a micro level. Proper strategic planning is foreign in most areas, but in personnel matters it is woefully inadequate. High degrees of human capital are crucial to good government, but not only does government frequently not have enough of the skills it requires at present, seldom does it plan to get them in the future. Often the only way to keep people with specific expertise is through appointing them to management grades irrespective of their ability to perform at these levels. Grade inflation undermines still further any career path, creating inflexibility, resentment and contributes to further poor management.

Uncompetitive government is useless when it comes to rewarding good or firing underperforming employees. The job for life approach is incompatible with modern ways of working. Heavy unionization protects the inefficient, and makes it difficult to reward better employees. Habitually early retirement or retirement on medical grounds, at great cost to the taxpayer, is seen as the only way to dispense with people who are not required. Early retirement is itself a blunt instrument, as it is tough to stop good people with crucial experience from leaving when generous terms are made available. Why should bad employees do better than those who are talented and work hard?

Lack of expertise and capacity to manage projects, particularly in areas involving new technology and dealing with associated implementation issues, is a weakness that undermines most initiatives. Although these can be compensated for by the use of consultants and contractors, it is normally at far greater expense than if public employees had been able to do the job themselves. The use of external personnel, or those on short term contracts, in addition to existing staff, is no substitute for proper government labor practices. In many instances, to have employees managing and supervising consultants and contractors, while not actually doing the work, is extremely poor value for the taxpayer, yet it has benefits for the less competent government manager, while it permits him or her to take the credit for successful delivery, it allows the blame to be placed elsewhere if something goes wrong.

To address all this public service must undergo fundamental change. Winning government needs to be populated with individuals with exceptional management ability who are motivated and empowered to deliver excellence. The right people are champions of performance, missionaries for delivery and evangelists for innovation. Winning governments successfully answer the "what's in it for me?" conundrum of public service. They inspire and enthuse employees to give of their very best. They set remuneration packages to attract first class talent, to reward skills and acknowledge hard work. They seek to retain good people by paying properly and not just appealing to their sense of duty or by constantly tapping their reservoir of good will. Salary levels match or exceed those offered by the nation's most profitable corporations.

Winning government requires the creation of a structure that facilitates the most effective use of competition to define and supply services. It is naïve to expect most of those currently in management positions within losing government to introduce it. As described, the most certain way is to create a new government machine in parallel with the existing structures, which should then be shut down. What is envisaged is a very small cadre of highly capable executives, operating like a headquarters function of a large corporation. Staffing levels will be broadly similar between countries, running into a few hundred employees, co-located, and working together to maximize effectiveness. The size of government outside this center, varies according to a nation's population and resources, and the success of public organizations in delivering best value.

It is in the nature of competitive government that significant changes occur in staffing within certain areas. For instance, success in law enforcement reduces the requirement for police officers and support staff; achieving greater prosperity cuts the numbers working in welfare services, and simplifying taxation results in fewer tax inspectors. Set against this, providing first class education or outstanding social care requires many more people. Retraining, redeploying and releasing staff to be more productively engaged is a key part of the process. Accomplishing this in the right way, motivating rather than alienating public employees is a very big change management exercise. The knack is creating organizations that are lean and efficient, focused on the provision of best value, and capable of demonstrating their performance to others. Those managers and current employees who are displaced by the creation of this framework need to be given every assistance to find new employment.

Government must acquire highly skilled human resource professionals who plan requirements, and manage staff to best effect. Winning governments adopt the personnel flexibilities that are used in the private sector. Government employees are not special cases. Crucially good performance needs to be highly valued and seen to be so, bad should lead to dismissal. Winning government cannot be expected to carry underperforming managers and employees. The ethos of government is one that prizes excellence, and creates an environment where its delivery is not only possible, but happens as a matter of course. Competitive government gives the framework, but it is the commitment of good people that make the difference.

Summary

Winning governments are obsessed by securing the greatest value for citizens and businesses. They organize and manage in ways that enable them to excel, their focus being on what are the best possible outcomes, and then working backwards to deliver. Such governments embrace the latest technology, and use it to facilitate success. Not only are they continually benchmarking performance, they create opportunities for feedback and actively solicit involvement and engagement.

Whereas no country can avoid the pressures of competitive government, winning government does not happen accidentally or by default. To deliver requires the full and active participation of citizens, the leadership of politicians, and a transformation in the way government is administered. The creation of an enterprising and dynamic public sector that yields the greatest possible value is an undoubted challenge, but it is not one that can be shirked or denied.

WINNING POLICIES

Successful implementation of winning policies and programs is the raison d'être of government. Uncompetitive governments lose sight of what they are trying to achieve, and get bogged down, burdened by a failure to see the wood for the trees. The biggest waste in government is not bureaucracy, it is failing policies and programs that either have not delivered, or are way past their sell-by-date. Not only are resources frittered away, the opportunity cost in terms of good policies and programs that cannot be funded is massive, not to mention the scope for potential tax cuts that are forgone.

Essential is a firm grip on objectives and priorities, identifying which outcomes are most important, and knowing how to focus efforts accordingly. It is vital to understand the incidence and impact of cross cutting programs on the delivery of policies. In this context, it is wrong to see education, law enforcement and welfare as separate areas, when in fact, they are very closely related and need to be joined up. For instance, outstanding education can have a far greater impact on reducing crime, than hiring tens of thousands of police officers and building countless jails. Equipping people with the skills they need to get good jobs can massively cut outlays on welfare. Investing at the "front end" of problems and can avoid having to pay much more at the "back end". Policies should be formulated to best deliver desired outcomes instead of dealing with the consequences of failure. The effectiveness of policies is also influenced by progress in other fields, and the actions of others. Programs that were appropriate at one time, are no longer be as relevant or effective as technology changes. Responding to new challenges, and taking advantage of advanced technologies, is the stuff of success.

Competitive government is about identifying and building on good practice, not just within a country but from around the world. Some governments already do a lot better than others, but achievement can also be a function of time and place. It is important to recognize that the process is ongoing, and a bit like a smorgasbord from which countries should seek to select the best for their particular circumstances. The straight copying of policies and programs is probably not practical or desirable, but what is vital is that lessons are learnt, principles applied, and delivery refined. Inevitably attention is drawn to what has gone wrong but this should be seen in the context of confronting essential truths so that mistakes can be recognized and where necessary put right.

Winning governments ensure that their policies are delivered better, and give much greater value for money than losing governments. The substance of the following policies is clearly open to political debate, however the belief is that they, or a variant of them, are at the heart of programs that deliver winning government.

Budgets and taxes

Government expenditure should be geared to the fundamental objective of increasing prosperity. On the basis that most government outlays are funded by taxation, it follows that taxes should make people better off.

For winning governments, the fiscal proposition is simple and stark. Society should be made more prosperous by tax financed government spending. This idea takes into account the redistributive impact of government activity. For while some pay more in taxes than they narrowly receive in services and vice versa, the wider benefits of a successful country must advantage all. The corollary is that countries can be impoverished by their governments. Taxes are a cost on individuals and business. The extent to which they are spent on services that do not give value for money, that do not further the creation of wealth, makes a country poorer and its citizens worse off. The unpopularity of taxes stems in significant part from the perceived or actual waste that results as a consequence. Competitive government provides the framework to judge the success of government in maximizing the return from tax. Crucial to good government is understanding and managing the tradeoff between value being created by government and value being destroyed.

It is important, therefore, to realize that at some level of taxation, every government reaches a point at which the marginal value of each additional dollar in tax revenue turns from positive to negative. This is not an absolute figure; it is a movable feast. It varies and is dependent on a variety of factors, some within the control of government, others outside it. The issue for governments is not the overall amount of tax, it is their competency; their ability to give real value for money for the taxes raised, and within this, creating a tax regime that encourages competitiveness and promotes national prosperity.

Citizens and businesses must be in the best possible position to assess the creation of value. Common sense would dictate that if people thought they got value from government then they would be well disposed to pay higher taxes to get more of it. In basic terms, governments know that the tipping point has been reached when voters fail to support further increases in taxation and demand tax cuts. Likewise, when businesses are deterred from investing in a country, or start to relocate to other jurisdictions and engage in complex tax planning, the taxation limit has probably been reached.

Traditionally, increasing taxes was seen as the way to improve or introduce new public services. This has changed. In virtually every developed country taxes are either perceived as too high or high enough. The saturation point has been reached, albeit at varied levels, voters do not want to pay more taxes, and many want them cut. In countries where citizens have to work nearly half the year, in some cases more, just to pay for government services, the challenge is obvious. Losing government does not sell, and should respond by delivering a fundamental change not only in what it provides, but what it charges in taxes to fund it. The temptation for uncompetitive government is different; rather than reform, it seeks to blur the link between services and taxes by borrowing and tax obscuration. It tries to increase the perception of value by providing more without headline increases in tax rates to pay for services.

Borrowing has always had a place in public finances, and can, if used wisely for investment in infrastructure, be a prudent and sensible path to follow. Unfortunately, very rarely does this prove to be the case. For uncompetitive government, the allure of piling on debt to help sustain current expenditure is just too great to resist. It becomes a way to avoid making hard decisions about improving the competitiveness of government, and distorts people's perception of value. Whereas increasing tax rates might cause outrage, few people are aware of the money borrowed in their name to be repaid at some time in the future. Of course the borrowing mounts up, gradually an uncompetitive government amasses more and more debt and interest obligations, creating massive liabilities and curtailing flexibilities, but for today's politicians and civil servants that is someone else's problem, a crisis for the next generation, but not for them to address.

The other approach to funding uncompetitive government is trying to disguise the true cost of government, through imposing multifarious taxes, duties, levies, surcharges and license fees, underpinned with increasing complexity. The result is that people are simply unaware of the full amount of tax they are paying, and thus not in a good position to challenge the worth of the services they receive. If citizens think they are paying 25% tax on what they earn, their view of the value of government provision is going to be different, than if they realize they are actually paying nearer 50%.

Extra complexity costs. With every twist and turn, the demand for accountants and lawyers to prepare, and tax inspectors to scrutinize the tax returns, increases. The greater the horror of the forms, the longer the tax code, the more time and money is wasted in their completion. Inexorably it becomes harder for the ordinary citizen to comply, increasing the possibility of noncompliance. On the basis, however, that ignorance is no excuse, tax authorities have acquired intrusive powers to investigate the affairs of taxpayers, who normally do not have the resources to "fight their case" on anything like equal terms and face punitive fines if "errors" are established. Complexity also costs government money, as it expands the black economy, by creating even bigger incentives not to declare income.

Further, the more complicated the system, the larger the scope to exploit loopholes, and the greater the opportunity for professionals to reduce personal and corporate tax liabilities.

In the seventeenth century, Jean-Baptiste Colbert stated that "the art of taxation consists in so plucking the goose as to obtain the largest amount of feathers with the least possible amount of hissing." The danger with uncompetitive governments is that they are so intent on plucking, they seek to ignore or mute the hissing, and so don't know where to stop, ending up killing the goose rather than helping it to grow and reproduce, to create more and bigger geese for the future. Conversely, competitive governments listen intently to the hissing, seeing it as a mechanism providing vital feedback to help them deliver greater value.

Budgets must be determined by the competence of government and its ability to add value. A government which provides better public services has a bigger budget, but is more competitive than a government with worse public services that spends less. There is no magic level of public expenditure at which a country becomes competitive or uncompetitive. What there are, however, are a series of judgments and comparisons that determine whether individuals and businesses believe that a government is adding sufficient value for the taxes imposed.

Globalization ruthlessly exposes governments that provide relatively poor value for money, bad public services, high taxes and convoluted tax regimes, and ultimately make their position unsustainable. A vicious cycle ensues that increases the burdens on public services, erodes the tax base, and make it harder and harder for a country to finance itself through borrowing.

Conversely, it helps those countries that give greater value for money, enabling them to offer even better public services, and or reduce taxes, all resulting in increased prosperity. Moves to frustrate this competition by tax harmonization and worldwide taxation regimes are akin to using a colander to bail out a boat, and are doomed to fail.

In this context the challenge for government is to provide winning public services that are highly competitive, that attract rather than repel businesses and individuals. Policy must be clear and focused, programs delivered in ways that are both efficient and effective. As uncompetitive governments seek to be competitive, they need to increase the value of what they offer. Services become better and, insofar as government decides it does not give sufficient value, costs and hence taxes or borrowing cut. The process of assessing value can be facilitated by re-establishing the linkage between services and taxes, and through tax simplification.

Countries with high debt levels find that they are denied much of the political help that direct connections between services and taxes facilitates. This only increases the challenge; it does not make it go away. The extent of success in offering better value is not as visible, for although the service may be improved, any savings are largely eaten up by reducing the deficit or paying back the debt instead of tax cuts. Addressing the problem of debt is essential to deliver winning government. Heavily indebted nations struggle to be competitive, it being both a symptom and cause of underperformance. The irresponsibility of previous generations, cannot be allowed to plague the lives of future ones. Managing the debt – interest payments and repaying the principal – gets in the way of progress. In addition, the potential for unfunded obligations such as pensions to trap a country in the mire of uncompetitiveness mean that they too have to be resolved. The issue is one of timing and degree; the underlying reality is that uncompetitive governments, unless they change, are doomed to fail. Making the transition to competitiveness is virtually impossible if countries are shackled to the corpse of a losing government's debt.

The adoption of competitive government, especially for countries seeking debt relief or even defaulting, requires considerable international cooperation and coordination to achieve successfully. Competitive government cannot be pursued in isolation from monetary policies; the control of inflation and low interest rates are a key feature of prosperity. The interrelationship between monetary and fiscal policies is very evident, but most governments have sought to distance themselves from the issues by the creation of "independent" central banks and financial institutions. In this environment gaining the acceptance and support of capital markets and investors for transforming government is a vital element. This involves them coming to terms with their imprudence in lending to uncompetitive governments, a factor which in itself spurs the move to competitiveness as failing governments find it increasingly hard to obtain further funding. There needs to be a recognition that hastening the writing off of debt, as part of a commitment to become competitive, is a far better proposition than the protracted agonies associated with a slow slide into the abyss. Establishing appropriate mechanisms for debt repudiation, restructuring or repurchase by central banks is, for many countries, an essential precursor to the adoption of winning policies.

Assuming borrowing can be managed down or eliminated, and interest payments are not excessive and inherited obligations not too burdensome; increasing the value of government is normally be twin track process with better policies and programs combined with tax reductions. Although related to government's provision of vital services and its ability to add value, as a rule of thumb, high tax rates discourage initiative and enterprise. They put off investors from locating in particular countries, and make the products of that country relatively uncompetitive on world markets. Taxes on business which exceed the value of public services provided, take money that could otherwise be used to invest in creating more prosperity, either directly or indirectly through rewarding investors. Countries with lower personal tax levels give individuals more money to spend or save. They attract talent and encourage people to work hard.

The most effective approach to cut taxation and reinforce competitiveness is to do so in ways that assist the transparency of and accountability for public services. The clearer the relationship, the more it underpins the process of competitive government, and the easier it is to assess value. Competitive countries seek to eliminate tax obscuration and promote simplification. Not only do such measures cut compliance costs, but they may even increase revenues, as incentives and opportunities are removed to evade and avoid tax. Within such remodeled systems, nations look increasingly at the advantages of flat taxes and hypothecation, together with cutting corporate taxation or abolishing it completely. The logic of taxing businesses, when at the same time needing to encourage enterprises of all sizes to generate prosperity and employment, thereby cutting welfare bills, is seen as ever more perverse.

As with other policies, competitive governments seek, through comparative analysis, to create the best tax regime, with tax rates and collection procedures that are more attractive than in rival countries. While judgments are inextricably linked with the value government provides; how it chooses to tax and the methods employed, can enhance or diminish its overall competitiveness.

Education

A first class education system is a vital determinate of national success. It is the most important investment that a society makes for its future prosperity. The level of expertise, flexibility and knowledge present in the workforce is central to a country's competitiveness.

For an individual, education is crucial to maximizing life's opportunities, and has a direct relationship with his or her potential earnings. Instilling a lifelong love of learning and providing ongoing education is essential.

Winning governments ensure that their education provision is outstanding at all levels. They put in place a framework that adopts global best practice, and prioritizes resources to give schools, colleges and universities the funding they need to help students achieve their full potential. Few would challenge this analysis, yet it is remarkable how ambivalent some governments are to getting the most value from their investment in education. Indeed, it is a common feature of governments, that very little "science" has been applied to the return on education expenditure. Given its pivotal position, does spending more actually save money in other areas and increase revenue long term? Winning governments actively explore this relationship to enhance their competitiveness.

Education needs draw out abilities, not constrain or straight jacket intelligence and aptitude. Schools must find out what children are good at, then help them to be the best they can possibly be. The fundamental question that should be asked is not whether a child is intelligent, but how are they intelligent? The answer may not be convenient or cheap, but ensuring that children get the personalized education they need to contribute most to society and to maximize their opportunities, is at the heart of success in the delivery of winning government.

Government has long been involved with education, in nearly all nations it is the main provider at all stages. In most developed countries the taxpayer supplies virtually all the money for formal education, giving access to children irrespective of their parents' ability to pay. Even though they often devote similar levels of resource, the value obtained differs significantly. Likewise, within countries and localities discrepancies exist, and as a result, the competitive challenge is evident. Losing governments have systems characterized by a situation where skills are not improving in line with the rapid development of technology and the needs of business. If education is standing still or moving too slowly, prosperity suffers as corporations are driven elsewhere. Poor education handicaps business, especially if they have to gear their production to the abilities of the workforce, rather than the drivers of competitiveness. Despite ten to twelve years of schooling and tens of thousands of dollars spent on education, in several developed countries it is quite possible for children to graduate crippled by ignorance; lacking the vital knowledge that is essential to make a full contribution to modern society, or even to find the most basic form of employment. The income gap between the "knows" and the "know nots" is growing significantly. The less skilled occupations, roles suffering from declining relative wages, are lost to developing nations whose people are prepared to work for less. Education is much more than an academic exercise; children need to be able to get good jobs when they leave school. High levels of youth unemployment highlight failing systems and losing governments.

With underperforming schools, particular weaknesses exist in math and science, and even those who can do the sums, fail if they cannot read the question. In many countries, literacy is at unacceptably poor levels with a significant proportion of individuals not being able to interpret even simple written instructions. Nonacademic activities such as sport, physical education and team competition are in decline. Partly as a result, young people are becoming more obese, losing the valuable experiences of camaraderie and collaborative effort, to secure success. It is frequently the case that the majority of children receive an education that is not as good as it could have been, and that the talents of the brightest children are often held back by a system that fails to stretch them.

For society, education provides one of the best prospects of addressing other problems such as poverty, discrimination and crime. It should give children a passport out of the deprivation faced in inner cities, and inspire them to make the right choices. Despite the well-publicized initiatives of governments, a large gap exists between the educational performance of students from rich and poor backgrounds.

Uncompetitive governments have failed to resolve the issues, frequently blurring failure by relaxing standards and making it appear as if the system is performing better by dumbing down examinations. Fundamental problems range from inadequate teaching, poor curricula, weak or non-existent discipline, greater numbers of disruptive children who can slow those who wish to learn, and insufficient or no homework. Other causes include poverty, more single parents and broken families, the lack of parental involvement in education, a rise in the amount of television watched and computer games played, and even a pressure to take low paid jobs rather than study. All these need to be addressed, but ultimately it is improved education provision that is the key solution to many of these issues. There is a chicken and egg cycle that requires decisive intervention to achieve a successful resolution.

Second rate education systems are run at the expense of good teachers. They are overworked and undervalued. As elsewhere in failing public services, those who are committed are not rewarded but burdened with extra responsibilities and work until their performance tails off. Stress, bureaucracy and penny pinching conspire to demotivate and discourage even the best. Taking advantage of goodwill is not only unfair, it is no recipe for success. Poor teachers can be resistant to change, reluctant to learn new skills and complacent, others are just too nice to do the job properly. Their training, possibly, twenty or thirty years ago, has not kept pace with the demands of modern society. Refresher courses are insufficient to fill the gaps. Often those who go into teaching have poor qualifications themselves. Schools suffer due to restrictive hiring practices, and the labor problems inherent in dealing with underperforming teachers.

Schools are sometimes subject to experiments that are more closely linked to social engineering than the pursuit of academic and educational excellence; giving each child the best help according to their abilities is sacrificed in favor of more egalitarian principles, and establishing the lowest common denominator. Streaming is abandoned, achievement is decried and ambition is condemned. Political correctness takes over such as treating boys and girls the same, when often their needs are different. It is proven that boys require more supervision and discipline than girls to complete tasks.

Aside from moving, the vast majority of parents lack choice over their schools. Those that can afford to pay, or are prepared to make considerable sacrifices, can in certain countries, secure better education for their offspring. However, it is an indictment of the poor standard of universal provision on offer in some countries that significant numbers of parents feel that they have to pay twice, once in their taxes and then again in fees to private schools to get the quality of education they believe necessary for their children. Likewise, the growth in private coaching and tutoring is indicative of the problems within publically funded schools. These are competitive messages that should spark fundamental improvements rather than be ignored or even suppressed. The real tragedy is that the children of the large number of parents who cannot pay, are disadvantaged for their whole lives, and society is all the poorer as a result. In many instances, private schools are not actually much more expensive than many state schools, when their full costs are calculated (especially if that sum includes consequent expenditure in other areas such as law enforcement and welfare), and normally succeed far better when it comes to delivering results.

Education is one of those fields where failure is incremental, but once it takes hold it can take a very long time to put it right, potentially affecting a whole generation. The consequences for competitiveness are obvious, yet with the advance of technology and globalization, these disparities are visible as never before. Governments need to switch from a supply or input based approach, favoring teachers and infrastructure, to a demand led, outcome view; focusing on the needs of the children and employers, their actual achievement and maximizing the value of taxpayer funding.

Education is the top priority for winning governments. Examining the systems of the countries that give the best education, and the performance of outstanding public and private schools, key principles emerge. These include: raising the status of teachers, paying and rewarding them accordingly, low pupil/teacher ratios with small class sizes, a concentration on the basic educational building blocks, selection to tailor schooling to children's abilities, high expectations, strong leadership from the head teacher and choice, competition and parental involvement. Schools that work best, inspire, praise and motivate children of all talents, they allow specialization and reward excellence, achieving a far better performance than those, which adopt a one size fits all approach. Rigorous attention to reading, writing and math supply an essential grounding for the development of work skills such as observing, listening, analyzing, measuring, estimating, calculating and presenting. Children are shown why subjects are relevant, with material presented in ways that spur interest and encourage active engagement. Curricula are geared to making sense of the modern world, and how pupils can best seize the opportunities it presents. They give the ability to use the latest technology, to manage information, to draw conclusions and make decisions. Schools include music, physical education and competitive sport in the curriculum, while offering a broad range of extra curricula activities, producing rounded individuals who can fully contribute to all aspects of society. In place of the retrospective school report, each child has an agreed Personal Development Plan setting out specific targets and how they are to be achieved. Smarter education technologies tie teaching to a child's individual needs, and facilitate the best use of local resources and global expertise. Lengthening the school day, increasing the duration of semesters and pre-school provision, not only gives children better education, but help working parents with childcare arrangements.

Winning education is closely aligned with the skills required by the labor market. This means engaging with corporations to blend on-the-job training with classroom activity. It requires a vocational approach, with tests and exams linked to portable qualifications and certifications that equip students to secure jobs. Internships and apprenticeships give work place experience and an understanding of the relevance of education to getting good employment, helping students and employers alike. To ensure effectiveness, choice and competition within the school system are very important. Empowering parents to choose where to send their children, through giving control over funding, helps improve standards. Freeing schools to manage, and to make their own decisions is a key element in this process. Learning from the finest schools and adopting best practice is central to progress.

Underpinning all this is money, while significant strides can be made without large increases in funding, really successful systems are fully funded to provide first class facilities not only for school age children, but to sustain learning for the wider community.

Education does not finish at school, winning governments have outstanding higher education that supports their future prosperity through the right mix of courses and degrees. Here an international market exists that successful nations exploit not only as a significant area of their economies but to help define their excellence. Attracting foreign students are hallmarks of good education systems, and have far wider benefits for countries than just the fees secured. Further education and universities are but one part of a bigger picture that provides lifetime support. The demands of a competitive economy require that learning is ongoing. Partly this is due to the rapidly changing nature of technology, but also to advances in health care that are inexorably extending peoples working lives. Winning countries make education available to help people learn, adapt and increase their productivity, regardless of age.

Health care

Developing a health care system that keeps people as healthy as possible, while controlling the costs is a fundamental challenge for winning government. Governments must also deal with the consequences of success; an aging population requires mechanisms to provide high quality social care, and give citizens choices as to when to end life.

Prevention is far better than a cure. Successful health care programs concentrate on ways of helping people stay healthy for as long as possible. Much of what makes people prone to illness is known; obesity, lack of exercise, smoking and alcohol abuse being the primary causes of early ill health. The reality facing government is that it is often politically easier for the health care system to treat patients with the consequent costs, than it is to persuade individuals to change their lifestyles, and avoid unhealthy behavior.

Advances in medical science and new procedures make it possible to cure more and more conditions, and although a blessing for mankind, they pose very difficult moral and value questions for governments and the current ways of funding health care. The demand for health care is fueled by its own success. As people live longer, they require more medical care. More medical care means that people live longer.

In most developed countries, health care budgets have risen very considerably. Since 1960 costs have doubled and the increase has been associated with a rise of about five years in average life expectancy. While it would be wrong to attribute all of this to medical intervention, on the assumption that this trend continues, and with current systems of health care, there comes a point when very hard decisions have to be made on what can be afforded, and for whom. Put very crudely, are another five years of average life expectancy worth doubling the money spent on health care? If so, as medical advances continue, the question emerges again and again. When does society judge that the demand for health care, crowds out other priorities and threatens national prosperity? Cutting-edge health care is a clear benefit, but it is also a cost that can make a country less competitive, as resources are sucked into looking after people who are no longer able to contribute, and whose quality of life is progressively limited. Hard though it is, societies have to make choices, what might be seen as compassion in one area, has implications for what can be done in others. The aim must be to use health care to keep people active and happy, and then to give them high quality care so that they can enjoy their retirement for as long as possible, creating a cliff edge situation at the end of life, rather than a steady decline.

How governments address the issues of health care help to define their competitiveness. There are many factors that come into play, but the costs of health care are huge, and the implications of failing to control it effectively are a vital issue. Even in countries where health care funding is not the direct responsibility of government, allowing costs to spiral out of control is not an option, for at some point insurance premiums become unaffordable for individuals and businesses alike.

It is important to analyze the effectiveness of different health care solutions, whether they are taxpayer funded, paid for by health insurance or a hybrid of both. Government sponsored regimes are very good at securing broad coverage, insurance based systems excel at giving high quality care. Universal schemes do not, in themselves, guarantee access when treatment is required, they are often plagued by waiting lists and delays, with certain forms of treatment not made available due to cost. Essentially, health care is rationed by doctors and administrators who have to live within the budgets set by politicians. Conversely, insurance systems can lead to excessive provision, treatment and cost. Hospitals can have significant over-capacity, and doctors recommend tests and procedures that are not strictly necessary. Those who are uninsured, predictably illustrate a fewer number of visits to physicians and hospitals. It does not mean that they are healthier, quite the reverse, with the delay in getting treatment actually making the medical intervention more serious and expensive when finally initiated.

Assessing the quality of treatment between systems is notoriously hard. Here there seems to be a tenuous connection between what is spent on health care and actual outcomes. In general, most developed nations achieve similar overall levels of performance, although this undoubtedly masks considerable differences in the patient's experience of health care. Measures such as customer satisfaction are also tricky because people generally tend to be more satisfied with relatively worse care, if they perceive it to be "free" and are not presented with an invoice at the end of their treatment. Facilities in government run systems can be Spartan and impersonal. With such regimes it is revealing the number of corporations that offer private health cover to employees, and individuals who take out insurance, prepared as with education, to pay double because of their government's failure to provide a standard of health care they consider acceptable.

The scope for the application of the principles of competitive government to health care is obvious. It is relatively simple to draw conclusions from analysis of life expectancy, treatment of dread diseases and overall cost. Why does this country manage to achieve similar outcomes while spending significantly less, why is that country so much more successful at treating that illness than another? The answers help determine which approach is the most effective.

Nations with considerable government involvement are the most effective at controlling the growth in health care costs. If one country can provide health care at less than half the cost of another, there appears a strong case for government participation. Yet this is not the whole story. A relatively cheaper government health system that fails to deliver, whether it be prevention, in-patient care, or the availability of key drugs is a failure of the government's promise, a betrayal which once sickness occurs is too late to rectify with alternative provision. Often such problems emerge in old age, and people's remaining years of life are blighted by substandard treatment. If private insurance companies operated in a like way there would be an outcry. Governments cannot be competitive by offering poor quality products. With patients becoming better informed about services available in other countries, and the availability of more effective treatments, relentless pressure exists for greater government funding. Ultimately, this generates demands that cannot be satisfied from public funds, and a new approach will have to be sought.

The solution lies with citizens – while government can create the climate for competitive health care – it must be left to individuals to make the decisions and provide the resources. Successful health care systems are ones in which there is a well-developed sense of personal responsibility for an individual's own health. This applies to adopting healthy lifestyles, to contributing to the cost of health care, and to ultimately making informed judgments about the termination of medical care and euthanasia when life is all but exhausted. Political skill is required to incorporate this within a system that provides the catch-all care that is the hallmark of a civilized society.

How is this to be achieved? First, and perhaps most obvious, individuals would prefer not to be sick in the first place. Helping people stay healthy is a key goal of competitive care and has major cost advantages over treatment. Systems must provide comprehensive health education and address the factors that contribute to premature illness. Success requires a much broader view that incentivizes healthy behavior and rewards individuals who take more responsibility for their own health. It is undeniable, for instance, that it is harder for those on low incomes to afford and prepare fresh foods. Tackling issues such as poor diet, obesity, smoking, lack of exercise, alcohol and substance abuse extend beyond the narrow confines of health care. As a basic principle, however, there needs to be a clear linkage between an individual's decisions, the consequences and their financial wellbeing. In universal health care systems where treatment is seen to be free, there seems to be less incentive to act in responsible ways compared to those in which the costs of unhealthy lifestyles are shouldered, at least in part, by the individual.

An effective approach involves making people more aware of their health care costs, with lower premiums or taxes for those who pursue healthy lifestyles, while maintaining a system that provides comprehensive cover in the event of an accident or the contraction of dread diseases. Included in this model is the idea of excesses, deterring unnecessary trips to physicians and emergency rooms. The extension of encouraging personal responsibility is the use of predicative tests that permit doctors to target preventive measures at those segments of populations who are most likely to benefit. Employing smart technologies to monitor wellbeing gives new opportunities to detect emerging problems before they get serious. Such advances reduce or avoid the development of ill-health later in life, and must be encouraged by making results a pooled risk, not allowing them to be factored into individual taxes or premiums. The sequencing of DNA, coupled with easy access to the latest clinical expertise, allow personalized medicine to deliver far more efficacious outcomes.

Second, where treatment is necessary, it is crucial within a system of competitive health care that it is as efficient and effective as possible. To achieve this involves real challenges to the health care establishment and its vested interests. The old can crowd out the new, as maintaining inappropriate health care infrastructures consume resources which would be better used on innovative approaches to treating patients. In the past operations required significant stays in hospitals, whereas with the latest technology, procedures can either be undertaken as day cases or treated by noninvasive ways. It means moving away from the physical infrastructure of treatment; hospitals, physicians, nurses and support staff and more toward what gives the best resolution for the patient. Systems that offer the most value are results based, they reward health care providers who adopt best practice, delivering higher quality outcomes at lower cost. Empowering patients by giving them greater control over payment, and allowing them to judge value they receive as interested consumers, also defines successful systems. By helping to create the right framework, governments can ensure that both citizens and providers are incentivized to improve a country's health care and keep costs down.

Third, the long term care of the elderly must be properly financed. Here it is vital to appreciate the vulnerabilities of the age group, and to put in place a regime that prizes care ahead of cutting costs. Given that the ambition of health policy is to help people live long lives, it is perverse to "punish" achievers in ways that undermine their dignity and diminish their quality of life. Everybody has an interest in making sure that provision is as good as it can be. Various methods exist to care for senior citizens. The extended family in many situations provides the best solution, but in others it is just not possible or desirable. Keeping people in their own homes, preserving independence for as long as practical is another. Creating well-resourced campus like communities of older people with similar interests can not only open a new phase in their lives, it can fight the destructive and debilitating loneliness that can blight people's remaining years. All need to acknowledge that the difficulty in looking after the elderly can be compounded by diseases, such as Alzheimer's and the onset of dementia.

It is too easy for uncompetitive governments to ignore the challenge of old age or try to sweep it under the carpet. The tendency is to trim and minimize social care, to be complicit in paying low wages for what is very demanding work, encouraging a race to the bottom in the knowledge that, by their demeanor, complaints from customers are likely to be limited. Conversely, winning governments ensure that the highest quality care is available. Such care is outcome based, focusing on happiness and wellbeing rather than the more traditional time and task approach. Matching the interests of carers to those being care for is crucial, good relationships require that people have things in common. Success also requires the active and involved participation of citizens, making choices before they reach the age of needing care. It demands innovative approaches that maintain independence and individuality, together with the availability of properly trained, well paid and motivated carers for those requiring help.

Life is sweet but it is important to recognize that for some individuals there comes a time when it is no longer the best solution. Given that death is ultimately certain, do people want to be artificially kept alive when their quality of life has vanished and their personal dignity all but extinguished, and is it right from society's point of view that resources are 'wasted' on such an endeavor? On average people make the most call on health care in their last year of life.

Using medical intervention to end life, raises awkward ethical and philosophical issues which winning governments must address. Doing so means tackling subjects that uncompetitive governments want to avoid. Life can be ended actively or passively by the withdrawal or non-provision of treatment. Who should make these decisions? As with other areas, the best solution to this problem comes through encouraging greater citizen involvement and responsibility. Given the choice when healthy, most people would say that they would prefer a quick death over a long and lingering one. Finding ways to allow citizens to make this election, incentivizing and formalizing decision making, and creating a framework where it is possible, is a role that cannot be shirked by government.

Winning government also intervenes to limit the scope for litigation in health care. The potential for resources to be diverted into insurance, lawyer's fees and damages, instead of caring for patients is very high and requires government action to prevent. The consequences of failing to address this including encouraging the practice of defensive medicine, are not advantageous for the individual or national competitiveness. The presumption must be that physicians and hospitals are always trying to act in the best interests of those who they are treating, with deterrence against malpractice provided by the criminal rather than civil courts and cases requiring a higher burden of proof.

Winning health care is not about change for change's sake, it concentrates on how to realize the benefits of improvements in medical technology, ensuring the delivery of the highest quality of care within a system that is not only affordable, but actually improves a country's competitiveness. Leading the debate, and the ability to articulate issues in ways that win popular support and personal commitment, are an essential ingredient of progress. Virtually all matters in health care are highly contentious and emotive. The problem is that ignoring them does not make them disappear, they just get harder and the provision gets worse. Coming up with solutions is a matter of critical importance to individuals, countries and governments. Losing governments make decisions by default or omission, winning governments by choice and with the active participation of their citizens.

Welfare

Winning governments have low welfare budgets for the fundamental reason that the need to support large numbers of citizens does not exist.

Losing governments are awash with welfare recipients and enslaved by their welfare outlays. Being clear about objectives is crucial to the welfare debate. Is success in welfare defined as paying more welfare or less? At one extreme it could be argued that an effective welfare system would do itself out of a job. Ideally it would create a situation where nobody needed help, because all had sufficient income to live without support. At the other, it is possible to envisage a system where virtually everyone is entitled to some form of welfare benefit, the success of the government agencies being measured by the extent of coverage, and the total amount of payments made. It is in the nature of a government department to favor the second interpretation, the former would threaten its existence, whereas the latter justifies tens of thousands of public employees, big budgets and powerful ministries for politicians. The real point, however, is whether for most individuals, welfare checks are actually the best way to promote their welfare? It is here that by objective measures, many government welfare systems can be judged as failing.

Welfare programs have grown from very modest beginnings to a situation where, in developed nations, they take a very significant proportion of public expenditure. It is essential for competitive government that welfare works, and that waste, in terms of the loss of the productive potential of recipients, and unnecessary payments is minimized. For most countries this requires a fundamental rethink of their welfare programs, the aim is both greater personal welfare and large reductions in welfare appropriations.

There will always be people who need the support of others. The origins of modern welfare go back to the time when it was quite possible for people to live and die in abject poverty and misery. In every developed country, welfare has largely succeeded in creating an environment where this should simply not happen.

Those with disabilities and illnesses that limit their ability to work, require assistance to live with as much dignity as possible. First class provision for these individuals is a proud stamp of a winning government, yet often those really in need of help, suffer as the attention of uncompetitive governments is distracted and dissipated by the larger welfare picture.

Effectiveness in welfare has been watered down by the changing definitions of poverty. Essentially there are two views, one of absolute, and the other, of relative poverty. Absolute poverty is not having enough to eat, no or extremely poor housing, insufficient clothing, poor or non-existent medical care and generally lacking the necessities of modern life. Relative poverty is usually defined as anyone falling below a certain percentage of average income. It focuses more on the degree of inequality in the distribution of income, rather than those in serious need.

Instead of declaring broad success in dealing with absolute poverty, most welfare systems now focus on relative poverty as their measure. Not only does this justify a welfare bureaucracy, it ensures that despite whatever is done, "the poor are always with us". As society gets richer, the poor may get richer too, but they are still relatively poor and in need of welfare. The narrative runs that the poor are victims of injustice, that this should be addressed by income redistribution, principally the transfer of cash and other services from the better off. This approach dominates thinking in most modern government welfare programs. The way that poverty is defined in uncompetitive countries means that they will not succeed in significantly reducing welfare expenditure. Welfare can be seen as a program without a goal, or one in which the goal posts keep moving, so that the "game" can never be won.

Irrespective of where you stand on the definition of poverty, the problem is that there is a growing realization that welfare is not the best way of giving most recipients a better life. Welfare is not bad per se, but how it operates is actually failing to create a prosperous and secure future for those who receive it. Just collecting welfare benefits is not, and can never be, a satisfactory route to escape poverty. Living on welfare does not promote happiness but instead promotes dependence, it imposes constraints and encourages behavior that condemns individuals to continued poverty. Welfare claimants are often characterized by single parenthood, systematic educational failure, the lack of the work ethos, ill health and obesity, a tendency to suffer from or commit crime, and to be engaged in substance abuse. Arguably, welfare actually creates its own demand. For instance, do young girls in some circumstances see motherhood as an economic proposition, giving access to a range of benefits including a possible entitlement to housing? Significantly, since the expansion of welfare systems to provide support to single mothers, the number of babies born to those who are not married or in a stable relationship, has increased dramatically. Many other issues may explain this, but the availability of welfare is certainly a factor. This has been coupled with a decline in parental responsibility. Most absent fathers do not give sufficient support to their children despite the efforts of government to enforce child maintenance.

The fundamental problem is that welfare checks are instantly attractive, they meet an immediate need, but can easily be a passport to long term poverty. Once people are established on welfare it is very hard to get them off benefits; they are caught in the welfare trap. The initial financial attraction of moving into work can be extremely limited, with individuals effectively facing marginal tax rates, allowing for the loss of benefits and entitlements, which are far worse than those imposed on the richest individuals in society.

The central predicament for welfare policy is how to keep support at acceptable levels to avoid poverty, without providing sufficient benefits that encourage more people to choose welfare rather than work? As policy makers have tried, so welfare has changed from a relatively simple system, to a highly complicated morass that consists of volumes of rules and regulations. Means tested welfare expenditure has exploded. The number of programs have multiplied, offering a range of money, food stamps, housing, social services, and in those countries lacking universal health care, medical cover. Few claim to understand all these in detail, especially how they interact for particular individuals. Technology, instead of making welfare easier to administer, has allowed it to get even more complex, and the beneficiaries have become more bewildered and confused.

The notion that living off welfare payments is acceptable has taken hold in developed countries. Welfare is a popular program, politically attractive especially as people like receiving money from the government. Benefits are easy to introduce, far harder to reform and reduce. The splintering of welfare programs, with payments to millions of voters, including those in work, has created powerful lobbies who do not want to lose their "entitlements." Working families, who by no objective assessment could be described as poor, receive money in many countries. Recipients regard such payments jealously, they see it as something they get back from government, conveniently ignoring the direct connection to taxes, and the inherent waste of fiscal churning – taking money with one hand and paying it back with the other.

The challenge for competitive governments is to find ways to retreat from welfare, and introduce more efficient and effective methods of improving peoples' living standards. Change requires agreement on the definition of poverty, what defines success, and boldness in securing popular support for radical initiatives. Stepping back, the obvious answer is that countries with successful economies generate more, better paid jobs, so reducing the pressure to make welfare payments. Less welfare expenditure means countries can tax less, cutting taxes on business means that it can create more jobs, and reducing personal taxes can increase consumption, further stimulating employment. Getting people off welfare and into work starts a virtuous cycle that makes individuals and society better off. A quid pro quo of cutting or eliminating corporate taxation is a full commitment to employee welfare such as paying a living wage so workers do not need welfare top ups. These efforts need to be supported by success in other areas such as helping people acquire skills and the provision of widespread, affordable childcare. Addressing these issues are essential aspects of fundamental change.

Governments should not just pay money out, they must leverage payments to get the most value. Effective welfare programs address both supply and demand, moving away from passive to active welfare, helping people improve their lives, find employment and remove their dependence on payments. In this context time limiting the availability of welfare provision incentivizes people to work. A further dimension is the creation of jobs, requiring individuals to undertake tasks such as litter collection, grass cutting and public space beautification projects; making welfare payments more like wage checks, with claimants effectively employed by the government. In these situations, the government becomes the employer of last resort.

The general presumption of winning welfare policy and programs must be that the aim is not to make welfare payments, but to get people into a position where they do not need help. A key element is creating a system that always rewards earning money, as opposed to receiving welfare checks. Rather than requiring complex tests and bureaucracy, the focus needs to be on encouraging personal responsibility, self-certification, and an emphasis on partnership not dependency. Overall a cap should be set for welfare payments, with scope to ratchet this down to reinforce reform.

The provision of an effective welfare safety net is a characteristic of a mature society. It can help, and encourage people to take risks such as starting a business, as well as mitigating the consequences of misfortunes that arise through no fault of the individuals concerned. Good welfare is an asset to competitiveness, but bad acts like a sea anchor, dragging a country down.

Winning governments learn from, and develop international best practice. Progress cannot be separated from economic growth, but getting welfare right is an intrinsic element of creating a dynamic and prosperous society. Understanding the causal link between high welfare provision and uncompetitiveness is the first step, the next is putting in place measures that enhance the welfare of citizens by improving

Pensions

Winning governments have affordable pension systems encouraging private provision for retirement.

Few examples of what is wrong with the evolution of government are more glaring than pensions. Uncompetitive governments have sleep walked into a situation where they have given, or implied promises, that they have made no provision to deliver. The result is that without fundamental changes, the credibility of government is severely compromised, and generations of citizens will be bitterly disappointed. Indeed, aside from addressing the issues raised, it is worth questioning whether winning government has a role at all in something that can be more effectively delivered by the market?

The pay as you go system that most governments operate was relatively painless to introduce decades ago, when there was a large working population in relation to the number of pensioners. It is virtually impossible to sustain when there is a declining working population, and increasing numbers of pensioners, who are living longer. There is an incredible naivety about this situation, amounting to wishful thinking. Most people assume that government runs some form of massive pension fund. In this fictitious arrangement, the money people pay in taxes is somehow saved or invested for their retirement. When they come to retire they are entitled to a pension because they have paid in for it. What they are not told is that government has already spent their pension contributions on others, and their pensions are determined by what existing taxpayers are prepared to pay.

Rogue corporations and unscrupulous businessmen have been rightly demonized for raiding their employees' pension funds, yet it is something uncompetitive government does every day, has done for decades, and intends to continue to do into the foreseeable future. Not only can government's promise not be met, but worse, it deceives people into not making alternative provision when they still could, through private providers. Cynics will observe that officials and politicians have sought to protect themselves from penury by putting in place very generous, unfunded pension arrangements. Uncompetitive governments seek to downplay the pensions issue, shying away from the bold decisions and declarations that are required.

Reform is essential to make pension promises affordable and to provide decent pensions. Competitive governments are honest with their citizens, managing expectations, exposing the sham security of the pay as you go model and helping them make alternative provision, as well as, remain in the workplace for longer.

First and foremost, the age at which people can retire, and expect to receive a taxpayer funded pension needs to rise very considerably. There must be a formal linkage to life expectancy, with the pension age set a few years below the average age of mortality. This means that people will have to work much longer, not only to provide them with an income as they grow older, but to increase their contribution to covering the cost of those already retired.

Second, pensions should be significantly increased to reflect average earnings, and be sufficient for pensioners to finance their retirements without having to resort to welfare. Government should also help establish equity release schemes to give access to the value of homes, to supplement pensions without the elderly having to sell their property.

Third, every encouragement should be given to citizens to make their own provision while they still can, either through pension funds or other investments. In particular, people should be helped to leave the pay as you go system, with a consequent reduction in their taxes. Considerable assistance could be provided in this aim by improved transparency, giving different payment options and making contributions directly linked to the value of the pension to be received. Encouraging opting out is not only to give citizens greater protection, it is to potentially give them better value and a real stake in increased national prosperity. In many systems, the government 'return' is significantly worse than if the same money had been prudently invested. As a result people have a lower standard of living than might otherwise have been the case. The risk of investment is outweighed by the certainty of poor returns. The fundamental issue is whether government is best placed to add value, or can alternative arrangements give citizens a better deal, greater choices and a more secure retirement?

Defense

Winning governments ensure that their defense is commensurate with the threat they face; no more, no less. Over provision is a waste, under risks disaster.

Defense is like insurance, in one sense you can never have

enough, but you have to balance the risk with the cost. Governments would be truly failing if they did not provide an effective defense. They are also failing, however, if they are paying too much for an out dated defense policy that covers threats that no longer exist, while not making sufficient preparation for challenges that do or are likely to develop.

Understanding the true nature of the threat is imperative. The reality is that for most countries, the main threats come from nontraditional areas such as terrorist attack, religious extremists and separatists, armed bandits operating for profit such as pirates, and cyber-warfare aimed at disrupting or controlling a country's infrastructure, as well as stealing its commercial secrets and intellectual property. In this context only a very small number of countries or groups pose any real danger. These nations are usually headed by political mavericks who, while very adept and ruthless at clinging to power, do not present any significant challenge outside their own region. Their "rotten states" just do not compete globally. Likewise, terrorists are incredibly weak when compared to the resources of those they seek to confront. That does not mean that they should be ignored, far from it, but they do not justify the expenditure of billions and even trillions of dollars on defense. The defense posture of most governments is akin to using a sledge hammer to crack, almost literally, a few nuts.

In some areas the potential for larger conflict remains, but in these the presence of weapons of mass destruction is sufficient to deter war as a rational policy. Indeed, the task is more to ensure the proper control of such devices so that they cannot be used by accident or fall into the hands of unauthorized personnel, rather than making plans to employ them as part of some sensible military adventure. The age old game of global chess will carry on, the task of politicians is to see issues in perspective and that make certain that matters do not escalate and acquire an uncontrollable momentum toward conflict. New frontiers such as space require international collaboration to avoid them from becoming the battlefields of the future.

It is often said that generals prepare to fight the last war. Without the pressure of competitive government, the defense establishment opts for the "safety zone" of modeling provision on updating what was needed in previous conflicts. As a result, uncompetitive countries maintain a defense structure that is significantly at odds with their likely needs. Governments boast a paper tiger military that is able to provide all the pomp that goes with nationhood down to the martial music, medals and uniforms. They have invested in some of the trophy hardware of defense: ships, aircraft, vehicles, but have not thought through what they really need to deal with the threats they face. Not only is this very wasteful, but actually dangerously deceptive when it comes to effective defense. Typically, armed forces are out of all proportion or relevance to the probable threat, and yet be incapable of being deployed, in any numbers, outside a country's immediate borders to counter challenges to its interests. Faced with cost pressures officers try to keep the same force structure, just smaller, the same types of weapons, but fewer of them. The hollowing out approach has severe operational consequences. Weapons are preserved at the expense of cutting the provision of spare parts, maintenance and training. Obsolescence reigns, armaments may be possessed but they cannot be used, and if sent into action would soon breakdown and could not be fixed. The weaknesses are legion, ranging from strategic planning, command and control, logistics and supplies, intelligence, and even political will.

While it would be wrong to assert that armed forces are completely unresponsive to change, their problem is changing quickly enough to be competitive. Long term procurement programs are initiated to address a perceived need or to update a capability, circumstances move on but the programs are virtually impossible to stop. Changes make for delay, add cost and impair effectiveness, and cancellation is engineered to be more expensive than continuing. When weapons finally emerge they have been so tweaked that they have lost much of their original justification, giving substance to the witticism that a camel is a horse designed by committee. Often, projects are commissioned for reasons of mistaken national pride, rather than purchasing "off the shelf" the most effective and economical equipment for a country's defense. The result of faulty procurement is that forces can suffer from a lack of the most basic items required to operate, and are denied "cheap" cutting edge technology instead having to make do with outdated systems because their over budget "superior" replacements have not been delivered.

With uncompetitive governments, the defense establishment is not only top heavy, it has a complement far greater than needed to respond to the threat. Questioning the value of recruiting, training and retaining significant numbers in the military and support services when they are not needed, is obvious. At the same time, demographic trends in virtually all countries mean that there is a smaller pool from which to recruit. The challenge gets tougher as new weapons become more sophisticated and require superior technical skills to maintain and operate them.

The ability of the military to enlist the people it needs, and to sustain the morale of the ones it has, and avoid incipient boredom, grows harder and harder. Added to this, service personnel, their families and public opinion are increasingly averse to armed intervention; the idea of putting people in harm's way, of taking casualties and losing lives is very unpopular. While this is perfectly understandable, it poses practical issues. How do you deploy your forces without exposing them to risk? Yet if you cannot use them, do you need to have them, and how does their presence contribute to effective defense?

Competitive governments find the answers to these questions lie in completely revamping their defense policies. They appreciate that the price of new weapons systems is rising but the costs of mounting successful attacks are falling. Rather than struggling to retain the totems of an outdated military infrastructure, countries need to focus on the best ways of identifying, preventing and dealing with threats before they emerge. Not only is this far more effective, it is far less expensive than building and maintaining the capacity to destroy them later on. In doing so, not only will make their defense much stronger, they free up resources to be used more productively elsewhere. Such an approach requires hard decisions. Nations can develop an emotional attachment to their armed forces. The day to day focus of those in the military can be more on defending what they have, cutting themselves off from scrutiny in vast bases, behind rows of razor tape, than actually eliminating real adversaries.

Winning defense thinking ensures that a country possesses an excellent military. It is agile and flexible, nimble and responsive, appropriately sized to deal with the actual threats faced and to secure sustainable victories. It maximizes the use of nonphysical methods of neutralizing enemies and works with law enforcement agencies to defeat "criminals". It emphasizes the value of covert operations, including interfering in the "domestic" affairs of other countries to "nip in the bud" challenges before they present real threats. It stops proliferation adopting innovative means. It addresses underlying problems before they are dangerous and looks to remove the sources of conflict for the future.

Where force has to be used, it employs it early on, with decisive power and a clearly defined exit strategy. While unmanned weapons and robots will be increasingly evident, highly professional and superbly equipped personnel are needed for certain missions and must be capable of being deployed and working with those from other countries. This requires common standards with interoperability, logistics, communications and smart procurement. It means replacing outdated alliances, and building new ones that reflect current, and possible future challenges. Defense planners also need to embrace a much broader view of their role, working collaboratively to provide solutions to global threats such as: disease and antibiotic resistance, climate change and water shortages, religious extremism, the lack of or corrupted education, and even making preparations to deflect near earth objects such as comets and asteroids.

There will be those who challenge the analysis saying that as you can't predict the future, you should try to keep as large a force as possible to deter any form of aggression. Such a "blank check" view is a negation of judgment, and ignores the reality of competitive government.

Countries that seek unnecessary and inappropriate military might, effectively weaken themselves trying to achieve it. This makes them more vulnerable, not less. The argument is not about ignoring threats; it is about dealing with them in the most effective way.

Law enforcement

At the heart of successful law enforcement is crime prevention, stopping people becoming criminals. Winning governments consistently deliver very low crime levels, and be able to cut the costs associated with law enforcement accordingly.

No government will ever eliminate crime. What it can do, however, is to engineer crime out of society through effective policies. This is especially important as law enforcement and the criminal justice system is one of the most jealously guarded "monopolies" of the state.

Countries with losing governments are subject to rising crime and a general lack of personal security. This is manifest not just in the actual crime committed, but in higher insurance premiums, and a broad range of concerns that could be summarized by "fear". The costs of failing to deal with crime are massive. Added to the billions spent on the police and law enforcement agencies, are the billions that go on the judicial system; courts, lawyers, jails and probation services. Even these amounts are only a proportion of the total expenditure; if insurance, the costs of repairing criminal damage and replacing stolen goods, not to mention the trauma of the victims are taken into account, the figure grows significantly.

A society that minimizes crime, not only becomes a more attractive place to live and invest, it secures a massive competitive advantage over nations where it is more prevalent. Money spent on the crime industry is money wasted. Success means that much of the expenditure that results from the "merry-go-round" of crime is no longer be required. The aim must be nothing short of victory, to achieve a lasting reduction in crime and the "support services" associated with it.

Uncompetitive governments put far less resource into preventing crime than trying to detect it, arrest the perpetrators, convict and detain them. Faced with rising crime, the standard government response is input rather than outcome focused. Governments seek to build on the infrastructure of crime — more police, more jails — instead of acting to undermine it at its foundations. Investing in prevention has massive benefits to society, and is a lot better than dealing with it after the event. There are a number of ways this can be achieved, including removing the motivations for crime, better use of technology, changes in policing methods, and ultimately through the long term physical detention of professional criminals.

The key is prevention. Stopping people wanting to commit crime in the first place, and when crime is committed, denying those responsible the chance to perpetrate further offenses in the future. Understanding and dealing with the causes of crime is central to success. It is usually part of a much larger picture involving family circumstances, education, welfare, lack of job opportunities and factors such as immigration and social exclusion. Few crimes happen by accident. Understanding why people offend and giving them better options so that they avoid criminal acts is key. There are a multitude of reasons for crime ranging from drugs, through poverty and greed, to just boredom and the search for excitement. Most crime is what might be termed "economic", to get money to buy something the person wants. It is carried out because the rewards exceed the risks or because people are desperate and feel they have little to lose if caught. It is the case that high levels of crime are often concentrated, and undertaken predominantly by certain categories of males between 15 and 25. It is estimated that of this group, only a very small proportion are responsible for most of a country's crime. Perpetrators know that there is a slim chance of them being apprehended, and if they are, they will be treated leniently, and will soon be free to commit further offenses. Most criminals are guilty of far more crimes than they are arrested for and convicted of. For many, criminality becomes a way of life, a reasoned proposition that can easily develop from the transgressions of youth to a full time career. In this context, jail is an occupational hazard and even a mark of distinction, rather than a disaster not to be contemplated. Despite attempts at rehabilitation, once a person has been incarcerated, it is very hard for them to rejoin mainstream society and get a reasonable job. Returning to crime is the natural result.

Successful crime reduction policies target the high risk groups in specific hot spots. In this it is virtually impossible to downplay the importance of good education. It is vital to ensure that schools give vulnerable children and teenagers the opportunities and values that make them see crime as the wrong choice for a fulfilling and happy life. Efforts to prevent offending must include intensive programs to tackle domestic violence and bullying at school. Home visits and extended support are crucial to avoid the creation of the next generation of criminals. Attention should be given to the warning characteristics such as low attainment, impulsive behavior and hyperactivity. In particular, governments need to devise innovative ways of dealing with substance abuse. Getting children to understand the dangers of drugs, and to say no, is central to crime reduction initiatives. Much crime is committed to fund drug habits. Removing this market, partly through programs that free users from the grip of drug dealers, and through legalization, cuts into the motivation for drug related crime. The approach is not permissive; drugs ruin lives, but is driven by an understanding that through a combination of treatment, and efforts to stop people taking drugs in the first place, the pressure to commit crime can be significantly reduced. Alcohol education programs to ensure that young people use drink sensibly, and in moderation, are another aspect vital to cut violence and vandalism. Designing out crime by removing easy opportunities has a major effect. It involves using resources in relatively obvious ways such as ensuring that properties in vulnerable areas have better door locks and window bolts, improved lighting and visibility, and more surveillance. It requires tackling antisocial behavior early on and promptly dealing with its manifestations such as graffiti. The larger picture is one that creates an economy that wants young people's contribution and rewards them with opportunity, jobs and prosperity when they leave education.

The role of the police is crucial not only to deter crime by being very visible, but also highly efficient in catching offenders. Police visits to schools, schemes that encourage interaction between vulnerable groups and the police, pay real dividends.

Creating an environment where the police and young people are seen to be on the same side is the foundation for effective policing.

In uncompetitive countries, it is evident that the police have lost their way in preventing crime. Police officers are detached from local communities, considered remote and unfriendly. The over "militarization" of the police has eroded trust and the readiness to use force weakened respect. Instead of working with the people, police officers are regarded as acting against them, a perception reinforced by poor customer service, bad training, excessive bureaucracy and the whiff of corruption. Coupled to this can be the over-zealous policing of the non-criminal class, such as trying to catch people out over minor traffic offences in order to make money from fines, further alienating those whom the police are meant to serve. The result is that police forces can become less and less effective.

Preventing crime and even catching criminals can take up quite a small proportion of an officer's time. Police strength is seldom deployed sensibly, with resources spread across countries to reflect distributions of population rather than levels of crime. Although technically there may be hundreds of officers in a particular area, very few are actually available for duty at any given moment. Absence, old-fashioned shift practices, physically unfit officers, form filling, court appearances, doubling up of patrols, meetings and other duties, and recruitment failures all militate against police effectiveness. Added to these are skill losses through early retirements – many on spurious grounds, the poor use of technology, and the fracturing of law enforcement effort into different jurisdictions, agencies and territorial units.

Winning policing is about putting right what has been allowed to go wrong. Best practice involves restoring the partnership with citizens, to provide confidence that law enforcement is focused on reducing fear, whether that be from physical attack, property crime or traffic accidents. Public safety should be paramount and high citizen satisfaction the goal. Police officers must be seen to be approachable and respectful, attentive and competent, responsive and fair. Merging responsibilities, especially at a local level with Fire Departments and ambulance services, to create a First Responder service to help people in difficulties puts the police back of the heart of local communities.

Making law enforcement more dynamic is part of a wider picture. In fact, most local police forces have a good idea who are the criminals in their areas. This intelligence is reinforced by new technology and surveillance methods that make it much easier to target individuals, identify criminals and illegal behavior. The bigger problem is that the judicial process, in many nations, has become dysfunctional. If a police officer knows that arresting a known offender involves excessive bureaucracy, and even if it does end up in a conviction, the likely result is a non-custodial sentence, or one in which the person gets out of jail in a short time, there is very little incentive for action.

Judicial systems need to tread a fine balance between the rights of the individual and the rights of society as a whole. Too often, however, the system is overly protective of the hardened and habitual criminal. Manifestations of this include the time taken to get cases heard, during which the accused is probably out on bail and able to commit other offences, court procedures that give too great a latitude to the defense, and limits on what the jury can be told about the defendant's past. That said, the aim of winning law enforcement is not to create criminals. For first time offenders indicted for comparatively minor misdemeanors, considerable judgment needs to be displayed on the implications of giving an individual a criminal record. Its impact on future employability can make it a punishment out of all proportion to the seriousness of the offence and even encourage further criminality. Indeed it is more of an own goal when the potential losses in tax contributions and costs in welfare payments are considered. Further, in those instances where criminalizing is unavoidable, scope should exist to wipe the slate clean at the earliest opportunity.

Sending people to jail on short terms is a disaster. It is a tremendous waste of resources and often cements a criminal career. Rather than rehabilitation, inmates can receive further instruction in crime, and can become victims of the drug culture, if not already enslaved to it. Society gets very little benefit, if once they are let out, they immediately reoffend using skills that make it harder for them to get convicted in future. Restorative justice, making good for the crime or contributing to improving the community in other ways present a far better option.

Where prison evidently works is keeping hardened criminals out of circulation. On the basis that offenders choose to commit crime, and that crime prevention efforts have failed, there is little advantage to society in releasing convicts to reoffend. Given the stigma attached to criminality, it is not as if the vast majority of former prisoners are going to step into well paid employment. Successful law enforcement systems make every attempt to stop individuals embarking on a criminal career, but those who deliberately and repeatedly offend need to know that when caught, they will be spending a very long time in jail. An effective system allows for redemption, but in these cases, the bar must be set very high to avoid giving the opportunity for further criminality.

The consequence of this approach is twofold. First, it reinforces the deterrent aspect of crime prevention, but second and more importantly, it starts to break the revolving door of crime. If criminals are not released, then they can't commit more crime; the number of criminals at large falls, and crime declines. This benefits society in numerous ways, and enables resources to be better used in other areas. Government becomes more competitive and prosperity is increased.

Recognition that law enforcement is in serious competition with organized crime and terrorists, requires increased international cooperation and collaboration. Police forces need to be able to tackle migrant criminals with proper controls. It is one thing for a country to be successful at indigenous crime prevention, it is quite another to expect it to address the consequences of failures elsewhere. Criminal gangs are more likely to operate in jurisdictions which have relatively poorly performing law enforcement agencies, and to take advantage of disjointed law enforcement within and between countries. Effective strategies are needed to deal with cross-border crime and abuse of emerging new technologies. Winning governments find ways to act with others, with increased integration with defense and intelligence services.

For winning governments, the objective is not mass incarceration which is very wasteful in itself. The aim is to prevent crime in the first place, and thus to have a small number in jail. Success means that winning governments are able to make significant reductions in the cost and numbers involved in law enforcement, and the related professions, savings that can be used to benefit their countries elsewhere.

Civil society

Countries need a framework of regulations in order to operate efficiently and effectively. Winning governments ensure that these actively promote rather than hinder competitiveness, prosperity and employment.

The creation of a civil society has been a fundamental role of government for thousands of years. Civilization requires a body of law to regulate human affairs and commercial relationships. The ability to form, and, if need be, enforce contracts is at the heart of most transactions, and without regulation competition itself can be imperiled. The problem is that too many laws and regulations, along with the infrastructure that supports them, can hurt rather than enhance prosperity. Under regulation causes problems, over regulation creates waste and stifles innovation.

For countries with uncompetitive governments, the harm of the growth in superfluous rules and regulations is extensive, they are a canker that undermines national performance. The costs are not just explicit, they are implicit in the value of what is lost or no longer done because it has been made too difficult and expensive. They can amount to a hidden hand, government control by proxy. The challenge for competitive governments is to get the balance right between imposing regulation and relying on good judgment. It is also important to recognize that this equilibrium is not a fixed point, it varies according to time and place. In other words, rules that were appropriate twenty years ago may not be right today. Winning governments look for global best practice in regulatory affairs, and adopt ideas and processes that leverage effectiveness and minimize costs.

Laws, regulations and the number of lawyers increased very significantly in the second half of the twentieth century. The extent to which this proliferation has benefited society is far harder to assess. There is no clear understanding how much the additional costs of litigation, compensation and insurance collectively detract from national prosperity and wellbeing. Competitive governments get to the bottom of the relationship, ensuring that the burdens are more than outweighed by the benefits. This is particularly relevant, as it is in many areas the growth of government itself that has spawned the explosion in regulations to be policed. Small lists of basic rules have become books; books have become volumes. Regulations have been introduced with the best of intentions, but with little thought as to how they would work in practice. Rules ranging from environmental controls, to health and safety, from welfare provision to anti-discrimination have permeated all parts of society. Walls of regulation, protected and supported by countless regulated professions sap customer service and the delivery of value.

Judgment and pragmatism have frequently been replaced by tedious detail. Comparison is rightly drawn between the vast disparity in length and clarity between the Ten Commandments or the US Constitution, and with this or that regulation for bananas or cucumbers. National regulation has been buttressed with international treaties, ingraining still further the potential challenges to be faced in reform. Across the world hundreds of millions of words exist to support government rules and regulations, frequently supplemented by further texts to define the precise meaning of the words themselves. Unchecked law supplants common sense. Often the rules and regulations become so complex, especially where they interact with each other, that there are few who could claim to understand them in their totality. Full compliance becomes virtually impossible, and as a result people start to lose respect for laws and those who create them. Given that the intention of detail is to provide certainty and remove discretion, it is perverse that its impact is to promote a fear of arbitrary authority. If few comprehend the rules, who is to know whether this government inspector is right or wrong? Likewise, instead of avoiding loopholes, complexity creates them. Decisions are never clear cut, appeals are nearly always possible, and the number of lawyers keep growing and multiplying.

Effective government is undermined because inexorably its activities are mired by the regulations that it has introduced. The effort of getting things done by the book can take so long that progress and change give way to maintaining the status quo and inactivity. Priorities are surrendered to process. The need to follow and be seen to follow the regulations, can stop bureaucrats from being sensible and doing the right thing. Accountability and authority evaporate, officials hide behind the weasel words of only following procedures and obeying the law. In some countries regulations diminish government by creating a climate in which corruption can thrive. The idea that you need contacts to progress, that bribes and payments are required to grease the wheels, is anathema to good government. Perversely the regulations can also often have an opposite effect, thus environmental controls can encourage companies to seek green field sites, employment rules can deter hiring, health and safety rules can discourage charities from helping the disadvantaged, and disability legislation can lead to less provision for the disabled, not more.

Laws and regulations have also encouraged the emergence of a blame society where personal misfortune is seen as somebody else's fault. The search for large compensation settlements, often out of all proportion to what an individual could hope to earn, and with awards approaching lottery wins, has driven an expansion of litigation. Fear of being sued is a black cloud that hangs over more and more areas, it is a blight that collectively and personally reduces wellbeing. Alongside the massive extra costs imposed, the demand for lawyers and their high salaries sucks the cream of young talent into law schools, rather than channeling them into more productive activity. The ranks of politicians are themselves swelled by lawyers, who cynically could be said to have a vested interest in the passage of new laws and regulations. Drafting more laws, devising additional rules, litigating over the issues created is undoubtedly intellectually interesting; the question is, to what extent arguing over how many angels can dance on a pin head actually contributes to national prosperity?

Winning governments systematically act to reduce the volume and the complexity of rules and regulations enforced in their countries. Governments seeking to become competitive need to take a deep breath, step back and look at their legal and regulatory systems afresh. They assess the value of what has been put in place, how it operates and the extent to which it encourages, or impedes the creation of wealth. Such action should be seen in concert with the need to massively simplify the tax system, and cut the scope of litigation generally. The most radical approach is a bonfire of red tape. It is sometimes said that rules are for the guidance of wise men, and the obedience of fools. A starting point would be for governments to declare adherence to all regulations passed from a certain date as advisory, rather than obligatory. The temptation is to choose less radical approaches, opting to keep some and dispense with others. The challenge is to find a way of wading through the tens of thousands of regulations and deciding which is important. The problem is akin to finding needles in a haystack. The danger is that the process takes a very long time, costs a great deal, and may even produce further regulations at its conclusion.

Success requires considerable resolution, the achievement is a significant and sustained reduction in government generated bureaucracy. Its measure is not an absolute point but judged by its contribution to the creation of a more dynamic and responsive economy that generates further prosperity. The results translate into lower costs, which in turn mean greater competitiveness. Businesses are still answerable for the quality of their products and services, and have to provide goods that customers want to buy. Removing employment and health and safety regulations would not undermine an employer's fundamental obligations to their employees. Likewise discrimination on grounds of sex, race or disability is fundamentally against the interests of good business and common sense. Rules and regulations may prevent a small minority from making the wrong decisions, but are frequently circumvented by rogue employers in any case. What they certainly achieve is to require the large majority to engage in massive extra bureaucracy, increasing costs and hurting competitiveness.

For those who think that largely deregulated enterprises are a risk, there are a number of impartial guides, surveys, feedback channels, comparison sites, rating agencies, certification bodies, underwriters' laboratories etc., setting standards which successful businesses will adopt and follow. Competitive corporations have a vested interest in providing products that are fit for purpose. In most cases, government rules and regulations are an unnecessary burden rather than a positive asset to improve quality. The specifications required by industry are usually more up-to-date than those imposed by government. The focus of government regulatory activity must instead rest principally on the promotion of the benefits of competition, and the removal of barriers, not only for itself but for its businesses and citizens. In particular, this means encouraging choice, and giving the capacity, knowledge and freedom to secure the products and services that offer the best value for money. Regulations should act to improve the efficiency of markets for goods, labor and finance. High level regulation has a powerful role to play as a way of addressing market failures and helping countries prepare for future challenges. The consequences of such initiatives need to be properly thought through and assessed, but they can advance competitiveness at little cost and create a sensible level playing field that benefits all. Winning governments guarantee fairness and access to impartial justice, they ensure contracts for the provision of goods and services are not weighted in favor of the providers, to the disadvantage of consumers. Pages and pages of end user agreements, the exclusion of liability, the waving of legal rights, the required acceptance of binding arbitration clauses with adjudicators paid for by the corporations themselves, all mitigate against the citizen, eroding rights and responsibilities.

To become competitive, many countries require radical action as far as their legal systems are concerned. A legal system that is lean, mean and efficient is an essential aim of a winning government, and a vital contributor to national prosperity and success. Indeed, it can attract business in its own right as parties to a dispute can choose to resolve matters in such a jurisdiction. One which is bloated, expensive and racked with delays, actually reduces justice and retards growth. For countries already blighted, the challenge will be greeted with howls of protest from the lawyers, but change is a priority if government is to act in its role to protect citizens and enhance their prosperity.

The aim of law and regulation must be to support the creation of wealth and to make a country a more attractive place to live and invest. It should give confidence and certainty to commercial transactions, and provide an environment that supports and rewards good behavior between businesses and citizens.

Infrastructure

Winning government's success in ensuring the provision of public goods such as transportation, energy, communications, clean water and public health are crucial to prosperity. It also has a wider responsibility to facilitate the availability of affordable

homes supported by appropriate facilities; including schools, health care, arts, cultural, leisure and retail stores.

The challenge is to make good public infrastructure happen. It requires degrees of competence that uncompetitive governments usually lack. It is one thing to appreciate the importance of infrastructure, it is something else to deliver, maintain and ultimately replace it.

At first, much infrastructure development was funded by private investors, but gradually in almost every developed country, government has taken a large measure of responsibility. It would be wrong, however, to overstate this homogeneity, significant diversity still exists in the way public infrastructure is managed and delivered. The central issue for competitive governments is to establish what works best and apply it with vigor to ensure that their countries are in the most advantageous position to compete.

It is important to recognize that often public goods such as roads, rail networks, airports, power stations, grids, water and drainage systems don't just materialize as a result of market mechanisms; they require vision, finance and persistence to ensure that they are put in place and maintained. Private investors need considerable assistance ranging from planning and zoning, licenses, investment and guarantees. In this area political uncertainty and government indecisiveness is the enemy of progress.

Invariably the fundamental issue is the timescales involved, few corporations can undertake projects, if the payback period runs into decades. Government is, in theory, much better placed, but often struggles to deliver. Public infrastructure can suffer from chronic underinvestment, especially in maintenance, refurbishment and renewal. It can become a victim of disjointed government, with rival jurisdictions and accountabilities.

The short-term nature of the political cycle conspires against long-term programs to modernize and develop infrastructure. It is easy to see how this happens, for instance, the investment program or repair budget can be cut in one year, to bail out an underperforming government program that is very visible to voters. Few notice if repairs to aged infrastructure are put off for another year, and this or that is not mended as soon as it otherwise might be. The result of cumulative failure becomes incredibly hard to rectify even if a future government wished, or was prepared to make available the funding to complete the work. Expertise is lost and the capacity of corporations to step in is reduced as businesses dispose of plant and machinery, and seek work elsewhere.

Another problem can be the political kudos attached to high profile projects. Business cases are skewed, attention diverted and funds syphoned off from numerous smaller, less sexy initiatives that would have a far greater impact on economic prosperity. Even when investment is forthcoming, public infrastructure programs can be plagued with protests, increasingly from environmental groups. Decisions are delayed, costs rise and proposals can be still born. Infrastructure projects can also get hijacked, with money wasted on investments that tick a political box, but are not the best use of resources from a national perspective.

Some countries have sought to address the investment problem through privatization. For certain industries especially telecommunications and other utilities this has been shown to work. Not only is there more investment, customer service has improved and with prudent regulation it is possible to see both better value for money and profits being made. The key word is "prudent", experience illustrates that not only do many governments fail to run infrastructure well, they also find it extremely hard to put in place proper control. Corporations must be incentivized to resist taking advantage of their positions, using exotic financial mechanisms, and the securitization of future income streams, to derive abnormal returns.

A successful economy enables people to seek a better living environment, a key element of which is accommodation. The availability of affordable housing must satisfy the aspirations of citizens to improve their lives. Those on average earnings should be able to finance home purchase and secure an appropriate mortgage. Rents must not exceed what working people can afford to pay. Government has a responsibility through planning and zoning, to ensure that development land is made available in the right areas, and homes are built to meet demand. Communities require not just dwellings but a full range of local infrastructure which government has a role to ensure is delivered. Much can be achieved through intensification in cities and towns, significantly increasing population densities by demolishing old buildings in favour of constructing higher occupancy new.

The fact that getting infrastructure right is very difficult, does not mean that the challenge should not be taken up. Quite the reverse, it is a key area where government can add real value.

In the context of competitive government, it is easy to study the experience of other countries, see which manage to provide good infrastructure and learn from them. Infrastructure must not be sacrificed to ideology, what works is what's needed and securing the best value the crux of public policy. The skill is to translate observation into results. Quality is as important as quantity. Avoiding locking into old technology, favoring flexibility, adaption and innovation is elementary. It is almost impossible to downplay the role of smart technologies in getting more out of a country's investment by using its capacity better. They range from water and energy meters, through intelligent grids and distribution networks, to smarter roads with autonomous systems such as driverless vehicles in cities and trucks capable of making journeys at night, so cutting congestion during the day.

The nirvana for winning governments is to find ways that leverage public and private infrastructure to give an outcome greater than the sum of its parts. A starting point is to be clear about the infrastructure needs of a country, and to establish a plan and priorities for delivery. Piecemeal developments are likely to be far less successful than an integrated approach that seeks to maximize the synergy between projects. Not only should government involvement get new infrastructure schemes moving faster, it should help to reduce costs, agree charging and revenue streams, manage risks and underpin contracts to guarantee effective delivery.

Winning government ensures that its country has an excellent public infrastructure with first class transportation systems, energy supplies that are dependable, plentiful and affordable, and state of the art communications.

Commerce and agriculture

Winning governments define their intervention in commerce and agriculture by the extent to which they can add greater value. As part of this assessment, they commit to effective environmental protection.

Seldom does direct government intervention in commerce enhance national competitiveness. The simple reason is that government, by its nature, is not as good at running businesses as businesses themselves. In agriculture, it invariably makes food more expensive than it would otherwise be, corrupting the global market place, to the disadvantage of developing economies and even encouraging the production of the "wrong" sort of food.

Many governments around the world still "run" sizable enterprises. Normally these are characterized by losses and subsidies, bad customer service, dubious loans and grants, restrictive practices, protection, and products and services that represent poor value for money. Such ownership continues, often not through ideological dogmatism, but because politicians are too frightened of the political challenges that privatization would unleash. In particular, for public utilities, government also doubts its ability to put in place a system of effective regulation to deliver competitive benefits. The consequence is a distortion of competition, a drain on the taxpayer and a loss of value for the citizen. Similarly nationalizing failing businesses does countries no favors and gets in the way of competition. Winning governments adopt global best practice, and divest themselves of concerns that could be better operated as private businesses, together with obstacles to free trade.

Unless convinced of their competence, competitive governments move away from blanket intervention in particular sectors, attempting to pick winners and providing regional support. Despite some liberalization, often a battery of rules, tariffs and duties exist to "protect" industries from foreign competition. The result is that consumers pay higher prices, have worse products, and industries remain uncompetitive. That said enterprising government needs the vision to create new markets which improve national competitiveness and encourage corporations to deliver.

Regional policies seek to lure international businesses to deprived areas, but invariably, these efforts are doomed because the fundamental problems are not addressed. The perversity is, however, that such measures would probably not even be necessary if the tax and regulatory regimes, together with other government programs, were sufficiently friendly for indigenous corporations big and small. Countries with winning governments attract foreign investment, and stimulate domestic businesses as a matter of course.

If uncompetitive governments are hesitant in disentangling themselves from interfering in commerce, in agriculture they are recalcitrant in the extreme. Over the years and with the best of intentions, a system of regulation, control and subsidy has been put in place which is almost universally regarded as wasteful and inefficient. The result is a testament to the failure of government involvement in activities outside its competence and expertise. The emphasis on intensive large scale agricultural production can be harmful to the environment, it encourages the exploitation of animals and land, with the use of large quantities of fertilizers and pesticides that can easily become pollutants, spurring the destruction of habitats and excessive water extraction.

Instead of motivating farmers to adjust to the needs of consumers and the market, farming the system for subsidies becomes a normal part of a farmer's life. Good crops, bad crops, or even no crops are of little significance, farmers get paid so long as they fill in the forms. Systems are often riddled with fraud, corruption and simple abuse. In many countries, agricultural support has acquired the characteristics of a rural welfare program. Assuming that such an objective is necessary and desirable, it could be achieved more cheaply and effectively without the waste and inefficiencies of subsides. Despite all the acknowledged failings, most governments and politicians are incredibly reluctant to act. Given the political geography of nations, farmer's lobbies are very effective, and electoral considerations frustrate initiatives.

Winning governments withdraw from agricultural support programs, and farmers are expected to compete on world markets. Removing subsidies is done in a progressive fashion and coupled with interim measures to assist the rural economy. In conjunction, effective environment strategies are established to protect and enhance a country's natural resources and bio diversity. In developing countries, winning governments and international non-governmental organizations seek to promote agricultural programs in ways that successfully deliver increases in production, while mitigating the unintended consequences that so often blights initiatives. Learning from the mistakes of agricultural support in developed nations and adopting a partnership approach is an important element in securing progress.

Summary

Winning policies have common threads that must be woven together for maximum success. No program can be judged in isolation; each contributes to the whole. Getting the right balance is crucial, understanding the most effective ways to achieve outcomes central to winning government. A key factor is leverage, appreciating how to have the biggest impact, to get the "most bangs from the buck." Government is especially powerful as a facilitator; oiling the wheels, setting the direction, providing leadership and incentives, it tends to be weakest when it gets involved in the minutia of actual delivery. Knowing how to add the most value to tax dollars, and how best to multiply these benefits, define winning governments.

How do winning governments spend their budgets? Relative shares depend on measures of citizen satisfaction and their relative competence, what governments decide to do and what they choose to leave to others. What is reasonable, however, is to assume that education, and education related expenditure form by far the largest single element, followed by health care, pensions and welfare. Success in the delivery of objectives will means the latter is in significant decline, as are outlays on defense and law enforcement. Again there is no magic formula, but a clear recognition about what contributes most to achieving national competitiveness and prosperity.

The level of resource available to each government varies. Deciding what is essential and then prioritizing is key. The starting point is the simple observation that people spend their first dollar a lot better than they spend their last. The same is true of government. Dividing an existing budget into quarters, and working out what is so important, that if government had only 25% of its current level of resource, it would have to be funded, is far more than just an academic exercise. The process not only requires proper information on the real costs and benefits, it establishes the building blocks for adding another 25% of funding and then the next.

Competition is the framework required to assess the relative performance in existing policies and programs, but also to determine better ways of future delivery. If the evaluation is done properly, what emerges is not all the current policies and programs remaining, cut down into equal smaller slices, but a radical realignment that illustrates what is really vital and what is less important. Coupled with harnessing best practice, and innovative and imaginative solutions to get the most value, the results lay the foundations for improving the competitiveness of government. In such a process, the assessment of the real benefit added by the last quarter of government expenditure becomes highly visible, and open to considerable debate. The implications for competitive government are obvious: what if government could achieve the vast majority of its outcomes with only 75% of its current outlays?

Competitive government is not about cutting funding per se, it concerns using competition to help improve and increase the value that policies and programs give. While it does not follow, therefore, that total spending is less and taxes are cut, indeed taxes could rise with really competent administrations; it is manifest that winning governments offer a far greater return for each dollar spent than uncompetitive governments and have a considerably larger impact in increasing their national prosperity.

EPILOGUE

Competitive government is the philosophy for the ongoing delivery of efficient and effective government. Those that seek to resist it, will be undermined by technology, falling prosperity and ultimately popular resistance to still higher taxes and poorer public services. They will be forced kicking and screaming to become competitive. Once embraced, drifting away from competitive government's central truths condemn a country to relative underperformance.

Competitive government is not easy, invariably the level of inertia is proportionate to the size of the institution. For most, becoming competitive requires comprehensive changes in the nature of government, what it seeks to do, and how it does it. It calls for a new mindset that treats the causes of problems instead of their symptoms. Winning governments concentrate obsessively on achieving the best outcomes and securing the highest impact. Above all they use the power of competition in all its forms, and seeking to promote choice to add, and create value. Governments are so large and commitments so long term, that fundamental change requires time. Like a massive super tanker, changing government's course does not happen instantly and probably will take a generation or more to complete. The need is to embark on the process now, to begin to realize the benefits, and to maintain the enthusiasm and the commitment over decades rather than months.

The biggest gains come to those peoples whose governments start applying the principles of competitive government early and build on their achievements. The good news is that some are already showing signs of beginning. The bad news is that most have not even seriously thought about it. As with all things the challenge is actually doing it, rather than just talking about it. Leadership is essential; the ability to see the opportunity, to grasp the nettle and to propel a country forward is a crucial ingredient for delivery.

Competitive government is an ongoing process, relative and absolute. A high performing government must retain its competitive advantage, or it gradually becomes uncompetitive. Governments need to be constantly alive to competitive pressures and opportunities for there can be no standing still; policies and programs that are competitive today may not be competitive tomorrow. Competition begs agility, innovation and risk taking, it requires not just listening to citizens, benchmarking and seeking to improve current services, but developing new ones that anticipate future demands. It means focusing on what could be done, as well as on what is done; understanding how best to harness the resources and potential of government to give the most value on a continuing basis.

Winning requires the most radical action but, for many, becoming competitive has little merit on its own. Winning and wanting to win, succeeding and remaining the best, has unparalleled advantages for a country and its people. Winning governments deliver a package of services and benefits that are consistently first class. They pursue the highest possible citizen satisfaction in every aspect of their operation. The prize is excellence, it is what citizens deserve and have a right to expect.

Acknowledgements

I am very grateful to Lily for all the help and encouragement she has given me. For a book so short, it has taken an inordinate amount of time to write. She has been incredibly long suffering, and I thank her for her patience and understanding.

I am very keen to receive comments and suggestions, to contribute please go to **competitivegovernment.com.**

About the author

Chris Prior is a passionate believer in the benefits of good government. He has worked in government at all levels, seeing its problems and opportunities from different perspectives. This book is the product of his experience, and of extensive research into the operation of government and global best practice.

He lives in Oxford with his wife, Lily, their son Cosmo, and Norman, their pug.

Made in the USA
San Bernardino, CA
03 July 2017